T0063660

FAQs on Anxiety

FAQs on Anxiety

Simon Chapple

sheldonPRESS

First published in Great Britain by Sheldon Press in 2022
An imprint of John Murray Press
A division of Hodder & Stoughton Ltd,
An Hachette UK company

1

This book is for information or educational purposes only and is not
intended to act as a substitute for medical advice or treatment. Any
person with a condition requiring medical attention should consult a
qualified medical practitioner or suitable therapist.

A CIP catalogue record for this title is available from the British
Library

Trade Paperback ISBN 978 1 399 80028 0
eBook ISBN 978 1 399 80029 7

Typeset in Caecilia LT Std by Palimpsest Book Production Ltd,
Falkirk, Stirlingshire

Printed and bound in Great Britain by Clays Ltd, Elcograf S.p.A.

John Murray Press policy is to use papers that are natural, renewable
and recyclable products and made from wood grown in sustainable
forests. The logging and manufacturing processes are expected to
conform to the environmental regulations of the country of origin.

John Murray Press
Carmelite House
50 Victoria Embankment
London EC4Y 0DZ

www.sheldonpress.co.uk

Contents

Introduction

You have no doubt picked up this book because you are experiencing uncertainty or have unanswered questions about anxiety. Maybe overwhelming worries or fears have been negatively affecting you or impacting the life of someone close to you and you have decided that it is time to find some answers in order to better understand anxiety and, more importantly, discover what can be done to overcome it.

This book will provide you with the answers you need by addressing the questions you might have been too afraid or too embarrassed to ask. FAQs on Anxiety has been written in a way that will make it easy for you to dip in and out of specific questions or topics whenever you need an answer. You will find the insights that follow will provide you with practical advice, support, reassurance, straightforward information and a new level of understanding, without the need for you to commit to reading an entire book if you prefer not to.

Many of the questions and answers in this book come from my personal experience of living with and overcoming severe anxiety, along with the insights of members of my community and feedback from readers of my previous books.

Anxiety began to affect my life as a teenager and gradually worsened to a point where I was experiencing panic attacks and avoiding certain situations where I feared I might feel overwhelmed. I ended up developing a problem with alcohol as it seemed to be the only thing that gave me any kind of relief from the racing thoughts, constant worrying and negative feelings.

Of course, the temporary escape provided by alcohol wasn't a sensible solution and my daily drinking developed into a secondary problem alongside my anxiety disorder. In fact, alcohol resulted in my anxiety becoming significantly worse, yet it took me almost two decades to realize it and even longer to do something about it.

Eventually I began to look closer at my life and started to educate myself about the best methods of eliminating anxiety and finding lasting happiness. This took me on a life-changing journey of discovery and personal growth where I learned and developed some of the most powerful tools and techniques to stop anxiety in its tracks. With persistence and commitment I managed to break free from the tight hold that anxiety had over my life. My hope is that after reading this book you will do the same.

If I were to rewind five years, I would find myself in a place where my anxiety was out of control and heading off the scale. It was controlling my life and negatively impacting me in almost every possible way. I would now describe my anxiety as 'normal' – it no longer has control over me and I haven't experienced a panic attack in over three years. Of course there are still times when I feel anxious, but the feelings are no longer overwhelming or damaging to my sense of wellbeing.

I now work as a life coach and help people from around the world overcome negative behaviour patterns, including addictions, anxiety and depression. My hope is that by reading this book you too will be able to unlock the same kind of breakthroughs and positive changes that I have experienced in my own life and witnessed in the thousands of people I have worked with.

You can discover more about my own journey by visiting my website at www.simonchapple.com

How to use this book

FAQs on Anxiety has been written to help you easily find answers to difficult questions about a disorder that is often misunderstood and misdiagnosed. You can dip in and out of the chapters at any time, without needing to read the entire book, and you will quickly discover the answers you need. You will also find answers to questions that you may have never thought about asking or you might have felt too afraid to ask.

As well as providing fast and easy answers to difficult questions about anxiety, the book also provides a framework that will help you learn how to address the challenging symptoms of anxiety that may have been causing significant problems in your life.

I recommend that you begin to use a journal and make entries to gather data in order that you can track your growth as you experience breakthroughs and a new level of understanding from what you learn in the book. Over time you can reflect on what you have learned, how far you have come and measure your progress by tracking and comparing your mood.

Above all, the goal of this book is to empower you to change your life by equipping you with the tools, tactics and support you need to break free from anxiety and find a new level of peace and happiness.

About anxiety

In order for you to reach a place where symptoms of anxiety are no longer causing major interference with your life, it is essential to have a clear understanding of what anxiety is and exactly how it can present itself.

You might already be certain that you have a problem with anxiety, but no two people are the same. It is important that you get complete clarity on your specific triggers and symptoms in order that you can create a tailored plan that will enable you to feel empowered and equipped as you go forward.

What is anxiety, exactly?

Anxiety is a natural and perfectly normal emotional and physical reaction to a stressful or difficult situation. It is usually triggered by a specific stressor and will end once the situation has passed. The right amount of anxiety can sharpen our senses and moti-vate us to deal with challenging events, day-to-day problems and bigger life issues, but it can also become a problem when the strong feelings appear out of the blue or more often than needed.

Everyday anxiety might be triggered by worries about paying bills, relationship concerns or stress related to work. When we experience anxiety, it is common to notice heightened senses and feelings. Depending on the specific situation, people commonly feel self-conscious, sad, embarrassed or fearful.

Anxiety exists to protect us from danger by allowing us to react quickly at times when we feel threatened. Our ancestors relied on their fight, flight or freeze response to survive potentially life-threatening situations with wild animals, enemies and their environment. These days the same fight, flight or freeze response helps people react quickly when faced with danger, such as a car accident, confrontation or a medical emergency.

When we are faced with a threat or danger, our brain responds by releasing stress hormones including cortisol and adrenaline. These cause the strong feelings of anxiety and allow us to react to the situation by increasing our senses, energy, strength and physical functioning. However, this stress reaction also takes parts of our mind and body offline, because the response is designed to keep us alive in times of danger; it ensures that we have the maximum benefits where they are needed most. When stress hormones are released we might have an elevated heart rate to help us move nutrients and oxygen to our muscles, dilated pupils and tunnel vision to allow more light in to improve our eyesight and focus and a numbed response to pain until after a threat has passed.

A strong stress response might also eliminate any feelings of hunger, sexual desire or the ability to focus on anything other than the perceived threat. These responses are all helpful when faced with real danger, but if the stress response is being triggered when there is no real risk it can feel debilitating.

Anxiety becomes a problem when it begins to impact our day-to-day life in a negative way: for example, when we worry too much and feel unable to control the torrent of thoughts and emotions associated with an overly active stress response. This results in our brain reacting when no real threat or danger exists, causing the release of stress hormones and the associated physical anxiety responses.

I can clearly recall a time when I would lie awake at night worrying about the prospect of someone leaving a negative review online about my business. No matter how hard I tried, the thoughts wouldn't leave me and they would expand into catastrophic scenarios of my business closing down and me ending up bankrupt as a result of the negative online comments that hadn't even been posted anywhere. The discomfort would stay with me for days and during that time I would feel a sense of worthlessness and impending dread that would make me feel irritable and down. I would have difficulty focusing on anything else.

To outsiders these kinds of worries may seem irrational, but that's the problem with an anxiety disorder: people on the outside don't always understand how challenging it feels and struggle to know what to do for the best or how to provide support.

If you have been experiencing heightened anxiety, I want you to know that your feelings are real. I know how real they are, because I have felt them too. Anxiety is not an illusion or a trick of the mind. The feelings exist within you, often as a result of behaviours that you learned at a very young age.

➡️ How do I know if I have a problem with anxiety?

Everyone experiences anxiety, but not everyone has a problem with it. The experience of anxiety is different for each of us, and dependent on a variety of factors relating to our lifestyle, our past and our genes.

It is common for people who begin to experience heightened anxiety to believe that it is simply related to stress or other aspects of their personal wellbeing, but over time it becomes apparent that the worrying and irrational thoughts seem to be almost constant and no matter what they do to get rid of them, they won't leave.

When I began to pay attention to my own anxiety, I found that I was:

- worrying excessively most of the time, usually for days or weeks on end

- worrying about things that felt irrational and out of proportion with the perceived problem

- struggling to sleep because of my worries and racing thoughts

- finding it hard to concentrate at work

- avoiding social and work situations that might make me anxious

- constantly on edge, as though something bad was about to happen

- less happy, irritable, experiencing mood swings and feeling down often.

There were times when I also experienced physical responses including:

- shaking hands

- sweaty palms

- hot flushes

- muscle pains.

If you have noticed that you are unable to control your worries, that you are worrying excessively about a lot of things, and that when you manage to let go of one worry you find yourself focusing on another one, the chances are that you are on the anxiety disorder spectrum.

While this book might help you identify if you have a problem with anxiety, it is no replacement for a formal medical diagnosis. If you think you might have an anxiety disorder, you should consider obtaining confirmation, and a diagnosis, from a medical professional.

What are the signs that someone has anxiety?

The main challenge for people with anxiety is the constant stream of worries and thoughts that feel impossible to stop. We feel fear and stress in the absence of danger or a threat.

- What if I lose my job?

- What if my boyfriend breaks up with me?

- What if I get cancer?

- What if I lose my voice in the middle of my presentation?

- What if I forgot to turn off the gas oven before I left the house?

One common theme among people with an anxiety disorder is that many of their worries begin with the words 'what if'. These two little words can be the fuel on the fire of anxiety and result in us experiencing significant stress.

People with anxiety will often seek comfort and reassurance by asking advice from other people, but no matter how much they share their worries it doesn't resolve them. They will find themselves constantly on edge and the more they dwell on their worries, the bigger these worries become.

Some of the most common signs of someone with anxiety are:

- constantly worrying, often about things that seem irrational

- often feeling uneasy, on edge, nervous, restless or irritable

- feeling as though the mind and thoughts are driven by an invisible powerful force

- a sense of danger or impending disaster

- difficulty concentrating on anything other than worries

- feeling unable to control the difficult thoughts and worries

- avoiding people, places and situations that cause increased anxiety

- fatigue, hunger and tiredness, especially after an anxiety attack

- difficulty sleeping

- low mood and depression

- feeling self-conscious about being anxious

- butterflies in the stomach or nausea

- feeling dizzy, faint or passing out

- tingling or pins and needles, usually in the hands

- an elevated or irregular heartbeat

- increased blood pressure

- muscle pain or tension

- needing to visit the toilet often

- excessive sweating

- loss of libido

- teeth grinding (often at night) or nail biting

- fast breathing, breathlessness or a tight chest

- panic attacks, which can feel as though you can't breathe or are having a heart attack.

Just like most disorders, anxiety exists on a spectrum. You might have one or two of these symptoms or you may have experienced many of them.

Try not to get wrapped up in worries about how bad you perceive your anxiety to be. You are already taking positive steps to address it by reading this book. If you continue to move forward and track your progress in a journal or with an app you should soon notice positive changes.

Are there different types of anxiety?

The most common type of anxiety is known as generalized anxiety disorder (GAD), diagnosed when someone worries most of the time for an extended period, often about things that seem irrational to others. However, there are a number of other types of anxiety and it makes sense to be aware of them.

Social anxiety

People who struggle with day-to-day situations that cause them to feel shame, criticism, humiliation or embarrassment are suffering a form of social anxiety. A sense of discomfort can arise even in situations that may seem easy to navigate to an outsider.

It is common for people with social anxiety to feel incredibly self-conscious and anxious about certain situations. They might describe themselves as shy, however shyness is temporary, while social anxiety is constant.

People with social anxiety often worry that they are being judged, and might avoid certain situations because they fear making a fool of themselves.

Social anxiety can impact people in just about any kind of social setting or environment where they sense that they are out of their comfort zone. Some of the most common situations in which people experience social anxiety are:

- work or school situations
- interviews or meetings

- giving presentations or public speaking

- eating or drinking in public

- using the phone in public

- speaking to someone in a shop

- social events, days and nights out with friends.

Like all forms of anxiety, social anxiety is different for everyone and it may not occur in all situations.

Panic disorder

Any type of anxiety can escalate into panic or anxiety attacks, which can feel overwhelming, or develop into a recurring theme of anxiety. Panic attacks involve an intense surge of stress hormones that create fear-based anxiety as the fight, flight or freeze response takes over, causing the sufferer to become debilitated by the symptoms.

Panic attacks have more obvious physical symptoms than generalized anxiety and they often seem to come out of nowhere. Symptoms usually dissipate between 10 to 30 minutes after they first appear.

The main symptoms experienced during a panic attack are:

- racing or irregular heartbeat or palpitations

- shortness of breath or difficulty breathing

- tightness in the chest

- blurred vision

- feeling dizzy, light-headed or fainting

- sweating or feeling chills in the body

- loss of colour in the face, looking washed out or grey in complexion

- a tingling sensation or numbness, often in the hands or feet

- nausea or sickness

- shaking in the hands or body

- a real fear that you may die during the panic attack.

Most people will experience a panic attack at some point during their lives, but people with a panic disorder will experience them frequently and often out of the blue.

Phobias

Phobias are an excessive fear of some kind of object, situation, person, event or behaviour. People with generalized anxiety disorder are more likely to develop a phobia of some kind.

People who suffer from phobias can experience anything from mild anxiety to a full blown panic attack when they are faced with the object of their fear.

Twelve of the most common phobias are:

- acrophobia – the fear of heights

- aerophobia – the fear of flying

- agoraphobia – the fear of claustrophobic situations

- arachnophobia – the fear of spiders

- brontophobia – the fear of thunderstorms and lightning

- carcinophobia – the fear of developing cancer

- cynophobia – the fear of dogs

- emetophobia – the fear of vomiting

- mysophobia – the fear of dirt and germs

- ophidiophobia – the fear of snakes

- phasophobia – the fear of ghosts

- trypanophobia – the fear of injections.

Phobias often stem from an earlier negative encounter with the object of fear. In many cases this happens in childhood when it is difficult to have a rational understanding of a situation.

Phobias can also arise through genes or learned behaviour: for example, both my mother and grandmother had an extreme phobia of blood, and I witnessed them faint in the presence of it many times as a child. As I grew older I developed the exact same phobia, and also found myself flat on my back at the sight of a nosebleed.

Other types of anxiety

Other types of anxiety include:

- post-traumatic stress disorder (PTSD) – caused by exposure to extremely distressing events, the symptoms can be long-lasting and severe

- obsessive compulsive disorder (OCD) – sufferers experience recurring thoughts and a pattern of repetitive behaviour that feels impossible to control

- health anxiety (also known as hypochondria) – this is when people constantly worry about their health; they often worry that they are sick or that they will develop an illness

- anxiety induced by substance abuse or medication

- anxiety induced by another medical condition.

➡️ Do I have to be formally diagnosed with anxiety, or can I diagnose myself?

If anxiety is having a negative impact on your life, it will likely help if you have a diagnosis in order that you have a clear understanding of why you feel the way you do. This can help you find the best treatments and solutions and help you understand more about yourself so you can effectively manage the problem.

You may already have a strong sense that you have an anxiety disorder from what you have read in this book and there is no prerequisite for you to be formally diagnosed. You can also find plenty of online tools that will provide you with a good indication as to whether you have a problem with anxiety or not. Some of these tools are listed in the Resources section at the back of this book.

The main benefits of having a formal diagnosis for anxiety disorder are that it:

- may ease your worries about what is wrong with you and provide you with a sense of comfort and relief

- will help your friends, family members and colleagues have a better understanding of you

- will provide you with better access to suitable treatments, therapy and support programmes – this may include medication if appropriate

- may help you to help other people who are also experiencing anxiety – you will be able to spot the signs and use your own experiences to offer suitable advice

- will help you explain and evidence your condition to your employer if necessary

You might find a formal diagnosis significantly improves your quality of life as you deepen your understanding of yourself, build your self-confidence and explore the options for treatment that meets your needs.

Whether or not you seek out a diagnosis is up to you. There is no right or wrong answer. I recommend speaking to the people you trust if you are unsure, then weighing up the pros and cons before making a decision.

➤ What is the difference between anxiety and depression (and will I get depression too)?

Anxiety and depression are both perfectly normal emotions that people feel from time to time. However, they can both become disorders and each should be viewed as a separate condition in its own right. It is possible for people to experience both conditions at the same time and it is not unusual for people to be unclear as to which one they are suffering from.

Depression is a mood disorder that prevents people from enjoying life. It causes people to experience a loss of interest in day-to-day activities, and they may feel sad and hopeless most of the time.

Anxiety, on the other hand, is a stress response that is triggered by a perception of danger and driven by worry and racing thoughts. People with anxiety are overwhelmed by disproportionate worry.

Anxiety disorders and depression share a number of common symptoms, but also have traits that are unique to each. It is, therefore, important to ensure you are clear on what you are dealing with in order to avoid a mis-diagnosis. If you are unsure I recommend obtaining a formal diagnosis from a medical specialist.

The most common symptoms of depression are:

- low mood and a negative outlook on life
- lack of energy and motivation
- loss of enjoyment and interest in day-to-day activities
- difficulty with concentration
- problems with sleep or excessive sleeping
- a sense of helplessness
- a lack of hope, feelings of guilt or worthlessness
- suicidal thoughts or thoughts about death.

The most common symptoms of anxiety are:

- excessive and irrational worrying
- difficulty controlling thoughts and feelings
- elevated heartbeat
- tight chest or difficulty breathing
- feeling edgy, uneasy, nervous or irritable
- difficulty with concentration
- difficulty sleeping
- panic attacks.

There are effective treatments for both anxiety and depression. A qualified professional will be able to offer you advice about the best options based on your individual needs.

Is anxiety the same as stress?

Anxiety and stress are both emotional responses that can feel incredibly powerful and at times overwhelming. Stress responses are usually caused by an external trigger, such as increased pressure at work or problems in a relationship. Anxiety, on the other hand, is triggered by constant worries that tend not to go away even when there is no stressor present.

Both anxiety and stress can cause a range of physical and mental symptoms including mood swings, irritability, anger, sadness, insomnia, fatigue, muscle pains, headaches, difficulty concentrating and tension in the body.

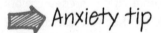 Is anxiety hereditary?

There is no single gene that has been found to cause anxiety, however combinations of genes passed down from parents can increase the chances of a child developing an anxiety disorder.

Studies have shown that anxiety is partly hereditary, but this aspect of the condition is far from the whole reason why people end up experiencing symptoms. There are numerous cases of people who have problems with anxiety who come from families with no history of the disorder.

Just because a member of your family has anxiety, it does not follow that their children will. The most important thing is to know the tell-tale signs of an anxiety disorder in order that you can find the right help and support for either yourself or a loved one.

Anxiety tip

Try replacing 'what if' thoughts with 'who' or 'how' questions. These will allow you to become more aware and uncover some meaningful insights. For example, the question: *What if I lose my job?* might become *How could I lose my job?*

Living with anxiety

Learning to live with anxiety is not about 'putting up' with the symptoms. It is about educating yourself so you can begin thriving in life by adopting a new approach and cultivating new skills and techniques that will allow you to feel a sense of freedom and calm, as you notice your anxious traits are no longer having the same impact as they may have done in the past.

In this section you will discover skills and techniques that you can integrate into your life to quickly minimize the impact that anxiety might be having on your day-to-day sense of wellbeing.

How can I live with an anxiety disorder?

As we have explored, anxiety is a reaction to stressful situations or experiences. You could consider an anxiety disorder to be rather like an early warning system for danger that is over-sensitive and becomes triggered when there is no real threat.

There are plenty of treatment options available to people who are struggling with anxiety, ranging from books, support groups and podcasts through to therapy and medication. It is important to take the time to find the right fit for your specific needs – don't assume that because the first method you try doesn't produce the desired results that nothing else is worth bothering with.

Living day to day with anxiety without a clear path towards recovery can feel like a challenge. It can seriously impact your mood and all-round sense of wellbeing and fulfillment. Obviously you could decide to do nothing and live as you are, but most people want to change and this involves making a plan and becoming clear on your goal.

People who are able to live happily and minimize the impact of an anxiety disorder have almost always invested time (and sometimes money) in themselves and worked on making positive changes. This isn't usually a linear journey, but with consistent effort and a determined attitude, most people are able to achieve significant reductions in their anxious feelings.

I believe that the foundations of change start by cultivating habits that allow people to become aware of how their disorder impacts them before educating themselves about the problem and introducing new positive habits into their day-to-day lives.

10 tips for cultivating habits that will help you change

1. **Develop an awareness of the problem:** Start to notice when anxiety shows up in your day. Pay attention to the times, locations and situations and start to explore each episode with a sense of curiosity by asking yourself why it is with you at a specific time.

2. **Keep a log:** Use a journal to track your anxiety disorder along with other metrics that will help you gather meaningful data. This might involve scoring your mood and your quality of sleep along with the number of anxiety episodes in a day. Your journal will allow you to bring mindful awareness to the problem and will also provide you with information you can look back on to notice how much you have improved.

3. **Educate yourself:** The more you understand a problem, the more power you will claim back from it.

Start to learn everything you can about your anxiety disorder from books, websites, studies and podcasts.

 4 *Know that you are not alone:* There are hundreds of anxiety support groups. You can find some excellent communities on Facebook and I recommend joining one and engaging as often as possible to ensure you feel connected on your journey to change and you have support on hand from people who understand what you are experiencing.

 5 *Find a mentor:* As you connect within the anxiety community, it makes sense to find someone who has achieved the same goal that you are working towards. Align yourself with someone who has overcome the same obstacles you will likely face and learn all you can from them. Don't be afraid to ask them directly if they would be willing to mentor you.

6 *Conduct an audit:* As you become more curious about what triggers your anxiety, it is worth conducting a thorough audit of your life. Pay particular attention to what people, places, situations and behaviours cause the biggest problems and then consider whether you need to make some changes or put boundaries in place to look after yourself.

7 *Be kind to yourself:* Eliminating anxiety is not an overnight fix; most people never completely eradicate the problem, but with persistence and effort many of them are able to significantly reduce the levels of anxiety they feel by getting things back to what might be considered a 'normal' level.

8 *Take baby steps:* Beating anxiety will likely mean that you need to make changes to various aspects of your life, developing new ways of thinking and forming healthy new habits. Don't try and do everything at once, or make huge changes before you feel ready; instead, take small steps forward and continually measure your progress and evaluate what is working and what needs adjustment.

9 *Explore the tools:* Later in the book we will look at some of the tactics and tools that have worked for me and thousands of other people who have beaten anxiety. Take the time to try them all and discover what will fit best into your life. These tools can be your saviour when anxiety strikes, and will also help you grow stronger and become more confident in your ability to make changes.

10 *Work on being more mindful:* The more you can become fully present and focused in the moment, the better. Mindfulness can be a huge help when it comes to reducing the effects of an anxiety disorder. There are many different ways you can become more mindful, you might consider meditation, breath work or silent walking, for example. Ensure you explore the options and gather the data so you know what benefits you the most.

Are there things I shouldn't do if I feel anxious?

If you have noticed that anxiety is having a negative impact on your life or holding you back from feeling joy and happiness, then it is important that you take the steps required to minimize the symptoms and ensure you can experience as much fulfilment as possible.

There are many different behaviours, habits and activities that could be ill-advised if you want to reduce your anxiety levels. However, everyone who suffers with anxiety is unique and it is our own individual responsibility to examine our lives and pay attention to what might be heightening anxiety.

There are a number of common things you should consider avoiding in order to make yourself feel better and to remove potential anxiety obstacles out of your own way.

 # Top 10 things not to do if you have a problem with anxiety

 1   Don't just accept it: millions of people around the world have successfully beaten an anxiety disorder – you are no different. Keep moving forward with the knowledge that change is achievable if you are willing to continue trying.

2   Don't eat foods that might elevate your stress levels: these can be the catalyst for increased anxiety. Later in the book we will look at nutrition in more detail.

 3   Don't expose yourself to unnecessary sources of stress.

4   Don't ignore the labels on any medication you take for other ailments – many medicines are known to heighten anxiety and could be contributing to your problem.

5   Don't get wrapped up in negative thoughts – most people who have anxiety feel frustration, sadness and anger, which can be exacerbated when unhelpful thinking arises. Learn the techniques for addressing negative thinking and these will help you manage the challenging emotions.

 6   Don't say yes to every social invite you receive. Just because you are invited doesn't mean you have to go – before you accept an invite, take the time to consider whether you really want to go or whether you feel like you should accept because of Fear, Obligation or Guilt

(FOG). If it is the latter, you might find the event won't benefit you and you may want to consider politely declining.

 7   Don't people-please – many people who suffer anxiety struggle to be truly authentic and often fear being rejected by other people. It is common for these types of people to try and please others even when it goes against their own values, wishes or opinions. If this applies to you, start learning about the best methods for becoming able to speak your truth.

8   Don't ignore your anxiety triggers – the things that can bring about strong feelings of anxiety. This can be anything, from a confined space to a song that holds negative memories for you. No matter what triggers your anxiety, make sure you take the time to understand it and if possible put boundaries in place to protect yourself.

9   Don't believe everything you are told about anxiety. When you begin to talk openly about your disorder you will find that people will offer you a wealth of advice and opinions. This comes from a place of caring, but the advice may not always be suited to your needs. Before you implement any suggestions, take the time to do your research.

 10   Don't go it alone. If you need help, and anxiety is preventing you from enjoying your life, make sure you ask for it. Later in the book you will find advice and information about the best places to find support and help.

It is also important to get the right mindset if you are serious about changing the way that anxiety features in your life. We tend to get exactly what we expect, so if you find yourself with a mindset where you are convinced that nothing will ever change, it is important to become aware of this, and to put some time and effort into learning how you can form a new mindset where you feel empowered and motivated to overcome the challenges you are facing.

⟹ How is my anxiety impacted by my lifestyle?

In the same way that where you live can impact on the levels of anxiety you experience, your lifestyle can also have a significant impact on how anxiety shows up in your life.

Many medical professionals and anxiety specialists recommend making lifestyle changes as an essential component of treating a disorder. While these changes may not completely eliminate anxiety, there is every chance that they will reduce the symptoms, and in some cases this can result in significant improvements.

An important aspect of overcoming an anxiety disorder is developing the ability to be totally honest about yourself by conducting a thorough assessment of your lifestyle and acknowledging whether certain behaviours or habits are making the problem worse.

⟹ 10 lifestyle changes you can make to reduce your anxiety levels right now

1 Exercise more: Exercise is probably the number one tool to help improve your mood and reduce the negative effects of anxiety. The results are almost instant due to the release of the feel-good effect of serotonin and endorphins, which exercise quickly produces in the brain. Regular exercise will also help you feel good about yourself, boost your confidence and can help you foster new relationships if you join a group or class.

 Change your diet: Even if you believe you have a good diet, there are almost always changes you can make that will provide you with more nutrients that will help reduce the effects of anxiety. Later in this section of the book you will find a list of the best foods for alleviating anxiety.

 Cut down (or cut out) alcohol: Studies have shown that alcohol can make anxiety worse, especially when people start to rely on it as a coping mechanism to self-medicate when they feel depressed or they are attempting to numb out uncomfortable emotions or feelings.

Remove stress from your life: It can be easy for stress to increase as we get older. When we are children we don't experience high levels of stress, but when we move into adulthood we begin to have responsibilities such as meeting mortgage payments, holding down jobs, navigating relationships and parenthood. It is no wonder we can develop anxiety disorders when you consider the amount of stress we encounter on a daily basis. Just because something causes us stress, it doesn't mean we have to accept it. Make sure you take the time to bring a conscious awareness to the stressful aspects of your life and consider how you can reduce the amount of stress you are exposed to.

Get cultural: You might be surprised to learn that people who engage in regular cultural activities experience lower levels of anxiety. These include trips to the theatre, museums and concerts.

Get creative: Similar to the positive impact of being more cultural, people who partake in creative activities also find that they have lower levels of anxiety. Creative activities might include painting, playing an instrument or a building project.

7 *Stop smoking:* Although it can feel as though it causes a short-term relief from negative feelings, smoking is shown to have a negative impact on anxiety. This includes regular cigarettes and vaping. Many people struggle to quit smoking and assume they aren't able to do it, but there are plenty of helpful programmes and support options available if you are serious about giving up.

8 *Become a mindful sleeper:* Many of those who struggle with anxiety also experience poor sleep. Constant worrying can make sleeping difficult at times, but we can make our own lives easier by becoming mindful about our sleeping habits. This involves tracking the quality of our sleep, maintaining a regular sleep schedule and auditing our sleeping area for anything that might be having a negative impact, such as a mattress that has seen better days, curtains that let light in or a quilt that is too thick for the current season.

9 *Avoid drinking too much caffeine:* Caffeine stimulates the fight, flight or freeze response which means it can be a big anxiety trigger. When I noticed the negative impact that caffeine was having in my life, I switched to decaf coffee and never looked back.

10 *Take a look at your supplements:* Just as you should read the label on any medication you take to check if it can make anxiety worse, do the same for any supplements you take. Many are promoted as 'natural' and sold over the counter, however this does not mean that they are suited to everyone. Some supplements contain significant amounts of caffeine while others contain ephedra which is known to increase the heart rate and levels of anxiety.

→ Can hobbies and pastimes reduce anxiety?

Hobbies and pastimes can be an excellent way of reducing the symptoms of anxiety as they have the ability to enable you to take your mind away from recurring thoughts and worries while you focus on something enjoyable.

The power of having a go-to hobby should not be underestimated and while it can be a case of trial and error to discover which activities feel like a good fit, it is worth putting in the effort to find out what works for you.

Some good hobbies and pastimes to consider include:

- **Craft-based activities**: For example, painting, drawing, photography, crochet or model-making. Any activity that allows you to express your creative side can be an excellent way to express your emotions in a healthy way while you become immersed in your creations.

- **Fitness and exercise**: When we exercise, we release feel-good endorphins and raise our body temperature. This can have a calming effect, make us feel happier and help to burn off excess energy that can cause anxious feelings.

- **Music**: Singing out loud and dancing are proven to improve mood. If you enjoy music, you might consider designating time to listen to more of what you love. You might also want to learn an instrument or join a group, both of which can allow you to express your emotions through the power of music.

- **Reading**: When we become immersed in a good book it can have a significant calming effect. Studies have shown a stress reduction of almost 70 per cent as people experience a lower heart rate and sense of relaxation as they read.*

---

* https://www.takingcharge.csh.umn.edu/reading-stress-relief#:~:text=Simply%20by%20opening%20a%20book,stress%20by%20up%20to%2068%25

- *Writing*: Whether you enjoy writing stories, journaling or crafting poetry, writing is a fantastic way to get out of your head and onto paper. When you are fully focused on your writing there is no room for anxious thoughts to enter.

- *Cooking*: Planning meals, making new creations and enjoying the fruits of your labour can be a lot of fun. When cooking is your hobby you will notice how you become lost in what you are doing and experience a reduction in anxious thoughts and feelings.

- *Gardening*: There is a huge satisfaction to be found in gardening and nurturing plants can provide a rewarding experience that gives a sense of purpose and fulfilment.

- *Animals*: If you enjoy the company of animals, you might be surprised to learn that interaction with them can reduce feelings of anxiety. If you don't have a pet of your own maybe you could volunteer at a rescue centre or offer to walk a friend's dog.

Does having anxiety make me an introvert?

Just because someone is introverted by nature it does not automatically follow that they will suffer from an anxiety disorder. Equally, those who are extroverts can struggle with anxiety problems too. However, anxiety is more common among introverts and my experience has shown that people can become more introverted when they are experiencing the symptoms of anxiety.

Many people try to keep the signs of an anxiety disorder hidden and develop 'high-functioning anxiety'. On the outside these people seem to be happy and in control of their lives, yet on the inside they are struggling with constant worries and negative stress responses to episodes and events that don't present a real threat.

High-functioning anxiety is usually driven by toxic shame which is essentially a sense of not feeling good enough in some way. At the heart of this is a fear of what would happen if we were to show the real version of ourselves to the world. The reality is that we would likely receive nothing but love and support. However, the perception of inadequacy and fear of being rejected for our self-labelled flaws can keep us stuck until we become able to face up to the power of speaking the truth, finding courage and asking for help when it is needed.

If you have anxiety and you identify as introverted, you may find that you have adapted your behaviour over time in a similar way to someone who is high functioning. Instead of hiding your perceived flaws from the world, you hide yourself from the world by becoming closed off. This is also driven by toxic shame and can be overcome by accepting and learning to manage your anxiety disorder. As the problem fades, you will find that your self-confidence returns and you are able to show up in the world as the authentic version of yourself, regardless of whether you are introverted, extroverted or somewhere in the middle.

It is important to note that many people are naturally introverted or extroverted, and just because someone has an anxiety disorder it doesn't necessarily mean this will change as the symptoms fade away. Very often our sense of self-worth, ego and confidence define whether we are introverted or extroverted, as you start to understand yourself better you will become able to take a closer look at this part of your life.

▰▶ Should I tell people I have anxiety?

The question of whether to share that you are facing challenges with anxiety with other people is one that comes up time and time again. When people are shy or introverted it can seem like a huge obstacle to overcome and it is important that you find a way to feel confident by having a plan in place that will work for you.

The same issue arises in my work as an addiction coach, people feel shame about their past behaviours and may have thoughts around whether they should tell other people they have become sober or not.

The traffic light system will help you quickly and easily work out who you should tell and who you shouldn't.

The traffic light system

This system is easy to use and will give you exactly what you need when it comes to working out who you should tell about the problems you have been facing with anxiety.

Whenever you encounter someone who you are considering sharing your story with, give them a colour, either green, amber or red, just like a traffic light. Once you have decided on the colour you can use the following process to know how much or how little you should share with them.

Green light: means that this person is safe and trustworthy, you can tell them pretty much anything.

Amber light: proceed with caution – you may want to share some of your story but be careful, if in doubt, say nothing.

Red light: this person can't be trusted with your personal information – maybe they gossip or judge others – whatever the reason, you have a sense that you shouldn't share and have given them a red light for a reason. Keep your story to yourself around these types of people.

The traffic light system is the perfect solution if you are unsure about how to tell others of your anxiety. However, there is also great power in being loud and proud about your journey. There is no shame in anxiety or any other mental health problem. In fact, most people will experience some sort of challenge to their mental health at some point in their life, and will feel inspired when they hear someone talking openly about the challenges they have faced.

You need to decide what feels like the right fit. If you want to start a YouTube channel and an Instagram account where you share your story and inspire others, go for it. If you prefer to share your journey only with the people you give a green light to, that is perfectly fine. There are no rules – this is about working out what feels right for your individual needs and then putting it into place in your life.

➡️ Are there good habits that help reduce anxiety?

Reducing the symptoms of anxiety starts with an awareness of the problem. If you can begin to pay attention to how you feel throughout the day, you will start to cultivate a whole new level of self-awareness that will help you understand yourself and your specific needs much better.

One of the best habits you can adopt is to name and label the various feelings and emotions that you experience throughout the day. There are several apps you can use to track and log these, and you can also use an emotion wheel to help you get really clear on the specific feeling that is with you at any given time.

By knowing exactly how you feel, you can learn how to meet your needs by seeing out the opposite of the negative or difficult emotion you are feeling.

- If you feel unheard, find someone who will listen to you – this might mean meeting a good friend for a chat over coffee.

- If you feel rage, do something to feel calm – possibly some form of relaxation or meditation.

- If you feel jealous, seek support and reassurance from the people who are important to you.

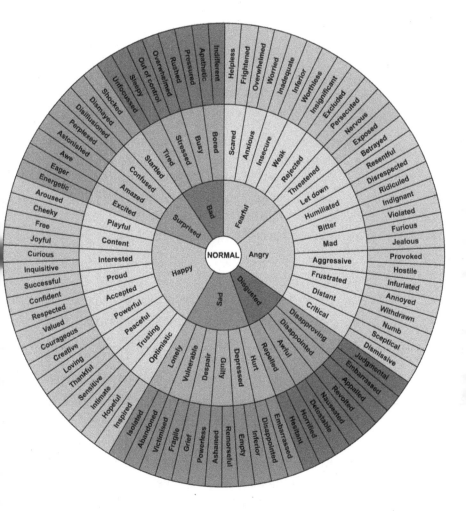

By simply taking the time to identify exactly how you feel, you will find that you become empowered when it comes to meeting your own needs, reducing the impact of anxiety when it begins to cause problems.

There are a number of other good habits that will also help you make your own life easier and minimize the symptoms:

10 good habits for beating anxiety

 1 *Exercise:* I make no apology for the repetition – exercise is the number one habit that will help you reduce the symptoms of anxiety. Create an exercise routine that is fun and interesting and make sure you stick to it.

2 *Meditation:* If you are new to meditation, I recommend using one of the many apps that will guide you through the steps to feeling calmer and more connected. You only need around ten minutes a day and once you begin to feel the benefits you will realize what an important part of your routine meditation should be.

3 *Social media and news:* Both of these are invisible sources of toxic anxiety – the more we can do to get in control of what media we digest, the better. You may not release how anxiety-inducing scrolling through posts that give an impression that other people have perfect lives can be. Equally, the sensationalist modern style of news reporting can have the same kind of impact, be careful what news and media you choose to digest, by being selective you can cut out some big sources of anxiety.

4 *Get into nature:* Spending time outdoors is a powerful way to reduce stress and anxious feelings. Whether you are walking, running or sitting in stillness, the natural environment is a mental health healer that will help you feel connected and grounded. A good habit is to get outdoors for a few minutes straight after you have woken up and again when the sun is setting later in the day, not only will this help with your sense of wellbeing, the natural light also assists by improving your sleep rhythms.

5 *Reward yourself:* Having treats to look forward to or enjoy will help improve your mood. If you link your rewards to the progress you are making on your journey to beating anxiety, then the treats will also help you stay motivated.

6 *Get the data:* By tracking your anxiety symptoms and recording the information, you will create a helpful record that you can look back on to see how far you have progressed, and it can also enable you to spot patterns to your symptoms. Many people use a journal and by writing a few paragraphs a day they are also able to process any challenging feelings and work through them by writing.

7 *Relax and rest:* Sometimes we need to take a break from the stresses and challenges of daily life. Pay attention to your mind and body and notice when you need to rest. You may find that a short nap helps you recharge, or relaxing for a few minutes with a book or puzzle helps you to get back into the right headspace.

8 *Sense of purpose:* When you have a sense of purpose it can feel like a powerful force that drives you to reach your goals, stay motivated and achieve what you believe in. Your sense of purpose will be unique to you and will usually align with your core values and individual needs. You can find a sense of purpose through work, hobbies, education, giving, wealth, relationships, physical activity and spirituality.

9 *Slow down:* Almost everything in the modern world is about speed. We demand faster deliveries, faster internet and faster service wherever we go. However this constant need for speed can come at a cost to our mental health. You have control of your own speed and intentionally slowing down is an excellent way to melt away anxious feelings. Get started by eating, walking and driving intentionally slower and notice how much difference it makes to your sense of wellbeing.

10 *Practise gratitude:* When we are experiencing anxiety, it can be very easy to beat ourselves up with negative self-talk and become convinced that life is terrible. If you take the time to write down three things you are grateful for every day, you will begin to notice the positive aspects of your life that you might take for granted. Use a journal to write down your daily gratitudes. Avoid choosing material possessions and instead focus on the small things that make a big difference to your life. For example, you will find things to be grateful for in many aspects of nature, your home and the people in your life.

Can non-anxiety medication make things worse?

Most medications come with a variety of potential side-effects and they can affect different people in different ways. Medication that interacts with the same parts of the brain and body as those that are activated by anxiety can be especially prone to causing symptoms.

When I was carrying out research for this book, I took a visit to the pharmacy to read the warnings on a selection of over-the-counter medications. I was overwhelmed by how many had the potential to cause anxiety – numerous pills, sprays and treatments all carried disclaimers of anxiety as a side-effect.

Some medications contain caffeine, which stimulates the nervous system and increases anxious feelings – for example, it can be found in medications taken for headaches and migraines.

From aspirin through to antidepressants, contraindications to medications are often hidden in the small print. If you are currently taking medicine to treat an ongoing condition, or you find yourself needing to do so in the future, I strongly recom-mend you research and double-check that your anxiety won't be impacted, and always discuss with your GP or healthcare professional before stopping any medication.

 ## What foods help reduce anxiety (and which ones make it worse)?

Nutrition plays an important role in maintaining wellbeing in both mind and body. By making some small changes to your diet, you can bring about some big rewards when it comes to managing your anxiety.

Top 10 foods to help reduce anxiety

 1 Fatty fish: Any fish that is high in omega 3 fatty acid will benefit your mental health. Salmon, mackerel, cod and sardines are among the best sources.

2 Complex carbohydrates: These are the ultimate anxiety-beating breakfast and lunch options due to their steady release of energy. They prevent the rollercoaster of energy highs and lows associated with sugary foods and snacks. Oats, wholemeal bread and pasta are among the best options.

 3 Asparagus: Thought to have anti-anxiety properties. In China, asparagus is used as a natural ingredient in the treatment of anxiety.

4 Leafy greens: Spinach, kale, greens or chard, for example, are packed with magnesium which can make you feel calmer and less anxious.

 5 Nuts: Walnuts, brazil nuts and cashews are high in antioxidants and likely to help reduce your symptoms.

Berries: Another great source of antioxidants are strawberries, blueberries, raspberries and blackberries. As part of a balanced, healthy diet, these will add to your anti-anxiety arsenal.

 Vitamin B foods: Grains, poultry, potatoes, bananas, eggs and dairy products are all good sources of vitamin B, and can balance anxiety and help ensure symptoms don't become overwhelming.

 Vitamin C foods: Diets that are rich in vitamin C can help us experience a better state of mind. Add oranges, broccoli and peppers to your diet to notice the difference.

 Probiotic foods: These are a type of super food that you should consider making a staple in your anti-anxiety nutrition plans. Probiotic foods are fermented and have live microorganisms that have a range of health benefits including reduced depression and anxiety. Some probiotic foods such as sauerkraut, kimchi and tempeh may take some getting used to as the taste can be quite powerful, whereas yoghurts and drinks such as kefir and kombucha are far more friendly on the palate.

 Chocolate: Yes, you read that right! Specifically dark chocolate, which has the potential to lower your blood pressure, and helps to improve the blood flow to your heart and brain which in turn reduces anxiety. Be careful though, dark chocolate also contains caffeine, if you overdo it you may find it increases your anxiety.

 ## 10 foods that can make anxiety worse

 Processed meat: This is associated with increased feelings of anxiety or depression. Try and minimize the amount of bacon, sausage, ham and canned meat that you include in your diet.

 2 Sugary foods and drinks: Numerous studies have shown the link between sugary foods and drinks and poor mental health, particularly depression and anxiety. These foods also increase the risk of diabetes, heart problems and a range of other medical conditions.

 3 High-gluten foods: These have been shown to increase feelings of depression and anxiety when compared to a gluten-free diet. Keep an eye out for the gluten content in your diet especially if you eat bread, cereals, pasta, biscuits and cakes.

4 Fructose foods: These are foods where the sugar has been processed to create a sweeter taste. You might see foods with high fructose labelled as containing refined sugar, sucrose or glucose. Pay attention to the packaging when you buy food as manufacturers can be creative when it comes to hiding unhealthy ingredients.

5 Phytic acid foods: Phytic acid is known as an anti-nutrient because it prevents minerals being absorbed into the body and stops us from receiving the nutrients we need. The more phytic acid you eat, the more minerals you block from your body. Phytic acid can play havoc with our wellbeing by starving us of the essential nutrients we need to feel good. Avoid seeds, beans, nuts and grains with a high phytic acid content.

6 Deep-fried foods: Chips and fried chicken are among the most common deep-fried foods. The process of deep frying makes the food high in saturated fats which can clog arteries and block a healthy flow of blood to the brain, which will further drive anxiety.

 7 Trans fats: These are found in cakes, doughnuts and cookies as well as fried foods and pizza. Trans fats are the worst kind of fat you can consume and they are responsible for the death of thousands of people around the world every year through their link to heart disease. As well as being a killer these fats also negatively impact mental health. If you are serious about beating anxiety, avoid trans fats.

8 Salty foods: Excessive salt is a recipe for disaster when it comes to mental health; too much sodium can play havoc with depression and anxiety. Pay attention to the amount of sodium in your food, it can be particularly high in ready meals, pre-made sandwiches, cold meats, sauces, fast food, dressings and pizza.

9 Processed foods or ultra-processed foods (UPF): These include foods that are frozen, tinned or dried and many contain very high levels of fat, salt and sugar which is shown to negatively affect anxiety and mood.

10 Alcohol: People who self-medicate with alcohol to manage an anxiety disorder are four times more likely to develop an addiction within three years than those who avoid using alcohol to numb anxiety. Alcohol is made with the ethanol, which is toxic, and as well as having a negative effect on almost every part of the body, it is also related to increased anxiety problems.

 ## Can my choice of clothing and furniture help reduce symptoms?

Many people who experience symptoms of anxiety come to the realization that at least some of their uncomfortable feelings have their root cause in a strong sense of insecurity they feel at times.

When we don't feel secure we tend not to feel completely safe. This is usually a subconscious feeling that goes back to the experiences we might have had as a baby. When a baby is wrapped up and warm and being comforted by its parents, it feels safe, but without these sources of comfort it can quickly feel insecure and anxious.

In adulthood the same principles apply. I am sure you can think of a few things in your life that make you feel secure. Maybe you have a soft blanket that you love to snuggle under while you relax in your favourite armchair, or a favourite spot in your garden that brings you a sense of peace and tranquility.

If you can bring about a mindful awareness of what makes you feel secure, you can cultivate your life to incorporate more of it. One of the best ways of doing this is by thinking about the clothing and furniture that you find yourself in contact with on a daily basis. If your mattress, quilt and bed sheets make you feel warm and safe, then they are doing their job well. But a lumpy mattress and a quilt that makes you feel cold because it is too thin for the time of year will have the opposite effect.

The same applies for what you wear. Clothes that fit well, feel comfortable and look good will boost your self-confidence and increase your sense of security when you wear them.

Take the time to audit the areas of your life that can impact how secure and safe you feel and don't be afraid to make changes or treat yourself to something new that will help minimize feelings of insecurity.

What else can make anxiety worse?

We all have our own individual template for the way we believe that things should be. This is what forms our expectations about the world and other people. When those expectations are not met, it can cause increased anxiety and stress, so it's important to know what your specific triggers are in order that you can manage them effectively.

Our expectation template is based on what we believe, but just because we believe something it doesn't mean that it is true. Our beliefs have been formed by the experiences we have had throughout our lives. We learn behaviour and replicate the behaviour of the people we trust and look up to especially as children. What we believe tends to stay with us into adulthood and many people fail to ever look at what they believe with any level of curiosity or inquisitiveness.

By bringing your beliefs out into the light and challenging yourself to see how true they really are, you will become able to access new perspectives and unlock new ways of thinking that will open you up to significant personal growth.

Many of the issues that make anxiety worse are linked to our individual template for the way we think things should be or may stem from other kinds of learned behaviour from our childhood. Take a moment to explore which behaviours apply to you in order that you can take steps towards change.

- Fighting negative thoughts: When we try to argue with negative thoughts or push them away, we tend to find that they expand rather than fade. It is true that "what we resist persists", and when we find ourselves fighting unhelpful thoughts, it is important to pay attention and learn how to beat negative thinking without an internal fight.

- Isolation: Time alone can be healthy and allow us to understand ourselves and our needs better, but too much time alone can have a negative impact and lead to increased anxiety.

- Feeling rejected: Many people have problems dealing with feelings of being rejected or abandoned. When activated, they can cause strong feelings of depression and anxiety. I struggled with this myself over the years until I realized that the problem came from my father who abandoned me when I was two years old. When I understood the root cause, I became able to take steps to heal the wound that I had carried into adulthood by educating myself.

- Loss of control: This is another behaviour that people can develop in childhood as a type of mechanism to cope with stress or frightening situations. While it may serve us as a child it can be debilitating and stress inducing as an adult. By paying attention to the level of need you have to control situations or people, you can begin to bring about a conscious awareness and take steps to change your behaviour and reduce anxiety.

- Lack of boundaries: We all have different emotional triggers – these can be people, places, situations or behaviours. They are very often symbolic of events from our past and cause difficult feelings, including heightened anxiety. If you can start to notice what causes your emotional triggers, you can put healthy boundaries in place to prevent you being exposed to internal upset.

- Validating your anxiety: When you believe your own negative thoughts and worries, you can increase your anxiety by self-confirming your fears and doubts. By adopting a mindset of curiosity you can start questioning your thoughts and exploring your feelings instead of moving to a default position of believing the worst-case scenario.

- Perfectionism: There is no such thing as perfection and when we spend our life trying to achieve it we leave ourselves open to significant amounts of anxiety as we drain our emotional energy on chasing something that doesn't exist. Learn to accept that nobody is perfect and become consciously imperfect so you can lean into the uncomfortable feelings and learn that nothing bad happens.

- Conflict: Fights and drama can be a huge cause of stress, upset and anxiety. If you can notice when you are becoming involved in drama it can be easy to step out of it quickly.

➡️ Anxiety tip

Work on accepting that there is very little in life that we can control. Start to put anxious feelings and stressful situations in perspective and use a journal to get a more rational understanding of them.

The emotional side of anxiety

Anxiety can affect people both physically and mentally. In this section we will explore the emotional side of anxiety and what you can do to manage your own mind so anxiety no longer feels like an overwhelming and uncontrollable force.

Is anxiety a type of emotion?

Yes, anxiety is an emotion linked to worries or fears, and one that is perfectly normal for you to experience. Anxiety can become a disorder when the concerns and worrisome thoughts become overwhelming or constantly repeat themselves without leaving.

How can I tell the difference between anxiety and fear?

Fear is an emotion that serves to protect us from threat or danger. Without it we would expose ourselves to all sorts of potentially life-threatening situations without any regard for the consequences. You may not realize it, but fear has probably saved your life on more than one occasion by preventing you from doing something dangerous.

Fear and anxiety often feel similar and it can be difficult to tell the difference. But there are a number of key attributes that set them apart from each other. The most important identifier is that fear will trigger us to take action to protect ourselves, usually in the present moment. Anxiety, on the other hand, tends to push away any desire to take action by repressing the underlying fear, since we perceive it to be an exaggeration or perception of danger rather than a reality.

The following table shows the difference between healthy fear and unhelpful anxiety.

Healthy fear	Anxiety disorder
A known or present threat or danger	A perception that there is danger
Fast reaction to a threat or danger	Constant worrying about a perceived threat or danger
Passes shortly after the danger has gone	Worries tend to repeat themselves
Always has a triggering stimulus	Doesn't always need a trigger to arise
Automatic response to the present	A reaction to the unknown or future
Helps us stay safe	Causes us to feel unsafe
Unlikely to cause long-term problems	Causes issues with mental health and wellbeing

Is anxiety linked to trauma?

Anxiety disorders are common among people who have experienced past trauma or had challenging childhoods. These distressing episodes can prompt changes in the brain that cause it to be much more prone to over-sensitive stress responses and anxious reactions to threats and danger that are not in proportion to the reality of a situation.

Trauma is a general term that describes the emotional response to a distressing event. Trauma sufferers often experience physical and emotional symptoms that can last long after the actual incident, these can include depression, shock, nightmares, flashbacks, migraines, insomnia, mood swings and withdrawal.

The types of incident that can cause trauma include:

- childhood trauma or emotional neglect
- violence trauma
- accident trauma
- domestic violence
- sexual trauma
- emotional abuse
- grief-related trauma
- bullying, coercive or manipulative abuse
- medical trauma
- military combat trauma
- natural disasters.

Many of these incidents can cause trauma symptoms either as a victim or as a witness.

You do not have to have been exposed to a traumatic episode to develop an anxiety disorder, but many of those who struggle with anxiety uncover some level of emotional neglect from their childhood or other type of traumatic episode that may contribute to the symptoms they are experiencing.

If any of this relates to you, have a look in the Resources at the end of the book for further advice and support.

How does anxiety affect my emotional wellbeing?

Anxiety disorders can cause a range of problems with our emotional wellbeing. When we are caught in a daily cycle of irrational fears and worries, it can be difficult to remain calm and grounded and many sufferers rarely feel happy or at peace in their lives. What may begin as a symptom of anxiety can quickly escalate into other kinds of negative emotional responses that can cause upset and problems for you and those around you.

Left untreated, you may experience more frequent stress-based responses and it is common to notice that the intensity of your reactions increases, which further impacts your sense of happiness and wellbeing. You can minimize the effect of this by paying attention to what is happening in your own experience: one way of doing this is to keep a journal and document the intensity, length, frequency and type of emotions you are feeling so that you can seek out specific solutions.

10 effects of anxiety on wellbeing

1 *Trouble feeling calm or relaxed:* The very nature of a stress response makes it almost impossible to feel relaxed or calm. Even when there is no obvious danger or threat, people with an anxiety disorder can find themselves feeling on edge or nervous.

2 *Low moods:* It is common for people with an anxiety disorder to experience low moods, mood swings and depression.

3 *Anger and annoyance:* Anxiety can leave people tired, frustrated and irritable, which can cause angry outbursts or inappropriate reactions to things that may seem minor.

 4 *Avoiding social situations:* Anxious people can stay away from friends, family and social events as a defence mechanism to try and protect against their symptoms. Ironically the lack of social connection can create further anxiety and perpetuate the problems.

 5 *Needing control:* It is common for people who have problems with anxiety to feel that they need to control everything in their lives. If you are anxious, control might serve as a defence mechanism to protect you from the underlying fears and beliefs that exist at the heart of your issues. Feeling out of control feels overwhelming.

 6 *Problems at night:* If you have a mind full of worries and unhelpful thoughts, you may well have trouble getting to sleep at bedtime, or you might find yourself waking up multiple times during the night. The lack of proper sleep means you don't enter all the cycles needed to feel fully rested and restored which can have a big impact on your overall mood and sense of wellbeing.

 7 *Self-confidence:* Anxious people tend to carry a level of toxic shame with an underlying subconscious belief that they are in some way not good enough. These unhelpful feelings can cause you to constantly compare yourself to others, which can make your anxiety much worse.

 8 *Withdrawal:* People with anxiety can suffer from a lack of motivation and you may withdraw from everyday activities that could boost your mood and sense of well-being. This could include avoiding exercise and healthy eating, for example.

9 *Relationship problems:* Anxiety can make it hard for people to maintain healthy relationships, and some partners find it particularly difficult, especially if they are unable to understand why their partner is struggling.

 10 *Authenticity challenges:* People with anxiety can find it hard to be authentic and may find themselves doing things they don't wish to do just to please others, and they might also find it hard to say what they really think at times. This can have a negative impact on their overall sense of wellbeing.

What does an anxiety attack feel like?

Also known as a panic attack, an anxiety attack can be overwhelming to the point of debilitation. These attacks are triggered by an intense stress response that causes physical, emotional and mental reactions. They can leave you feeling distressed, confused and worried after the symptoms have subsided.

Although anxiety attacks last on average for around ten minutes, it can take several hours to fully recover due to the overpowering feelings, emotions and reactions. The experience of an anxiety attack can be so strong that some people believe that they are having a heart attack and become convinced they are about to die.

Stephen, who has experienced anxiety for over ten years, recalls: 'The most intense anxiety attacks I experienced were related to my fear of blood. They became especially triggered when I felt trapped and couldn't get away from the source of my fear. Once, at work, a colleague was talking about her daughter having a nosebleed. She was standing in my office doorway. I was unable to get out and I felt the early tingling sensations of an anxiety attack building within me. I actually fainted and woke up on the floor staring at the ceiling. This doesn't usually happen, though – normally I would feel the attack coming, and soon my vision would begin to blur, the colour would drain from my skin and I would break out in a cold sweat. I would feel totally overwhelmed and terrified, with a sickening swirly, dizzy feeling of being out of control. My panic attacks were so frightening and I had no defences to fight back. I usually just gave in, and lay down on the floor until they passed.'

People who experience anxiety attacks may feel as though they can't breathe, feel sick, feel their heart beating hard in their chest while their hands and body shake uncontrollably.

Stephen adds: 'When I was experiencing an anxiety attack I found it helped to get cool air and splash myself with water. Sometimes drinking water helped me, as did sitting up and placing my head between my knees.'

Once the reaction has happened in the brain, there is nothing we can do to stop it. All we can do is work out what can take the edge off in order to try and help ourselves return to some form of normality as quickly as possible.

7 tips to use during an anxiety attack

 1 *Use visualization:* It can help to fix your attention on something in your mind's eye and focus on it until the attack has passed.

 2 *Breathing control:* Breathing in and out of a paper bag, or diverting your attention to your breath and consciously following it in and out of your nose and mouth, may also help you to move through an anxiety attack with less discomfort.

 3 *Lying down:* Anxiety attacks can cause dizziness and fainting. Lying down can help us feel safe and grounded and reduce the strength of the attack.

Remove yourself: Anxiety attacks are often made worse when we feel trapped and unable to leave a situation. However, you have the power and the right to remove yourself if you feel the onset of heightened anxiety. People will be understanding and if you don't have time to explain what is happening you can do so when the feelings have passed and you feel ready as it is important to respond before it becomes overwhelming. Take the time to know your 'safe place' as this can be your sanctuary during challenging times, you might choose to take a short walk or sit in a bathroom cubicle for example.

 Water: Splashing your face and body or drinking cold water can divert your attention and help remove some of the energy from an anxiety attack.

6 | *Use a mantra:* During an anxiety attack it can help to repeat a positive mantra to help you keep your focus in one place and remain as calm and relaxed as possible during the challenging experience. You could simply repeat 'everything passes' over and over either out loud or in your head until the strong feelings start to fade.

7 | *The 5-4-3-2-1 technique:* A simple technique that can help you stay grounded and fully present during an anxiety attack is to focus on what is around you by intentionally connecting with each of your five senses, do this by noticing:

5 things you can see
4 things you can touch
3 things you can hear
2 things you can smell
1 thing you can taste

➡ Can an anxiety attack cause a heart attack?

Many people who experience an anxiety attack feel tightness in their chest or a shortness of breath. Couple this with the intensity of the experience and this can cause you to believe you may be having a heart attack. The feeling of an anxiety attack can be frightening, but please be assured that it cannot cause a heart attack.

➡ Why is my brain constantly racing with thoughts?

If you have an anxiety disorder, you might feel as though your mind has become a constant stream of worrying thoughts. The incessant chatter disrupts your wellbeing, because it becomes almost impossible to feel any sense of peace or calm with a brain that seems to be permanently on alert.

Such racing thoughts are one of the symptoms of anxiety. Maya says: 'In my own experience, I found that even when I was able to calm down a particularly challenging thought, it wouldn't take long before I latched onto the next one and the worries would escalate all over again.'

While racing thoughts are common among people who suffer with anxiety they are also a symptom of:

- attention deficit hyperactivity disorder (ADHD)
- depression
- bipolar disorder (BPD)
- obsessive compulsive disorder (OCD).

It is possible to get back in control and calm down a racing mind. Maya reflects: 'I found meditation to be particularly helpful and to this day I still ensure I use an app each morning and evening for a ten minute practice as it helps to keep me grounded, calm and centred.'

Other kinds of breathing exercises can also help, as can journaling and medication.

➡ Are people with anxiety negative thinkers?

If you have experienced anxiety, you will no doubt already be aware that negative thoughts in the form of worries and fears are a major symptom of the disorder. You might believe it follows that people with anxiety must be negative thinkers by default.

This isn't necessarily true. When people with anxiety disorders are able to break free from their negative thought patterns they almost always grow in self-confidence, with a sense of personal value and worthiness that results in them having a much more positive outlook on life.

It is also common for people with an anxiety problem to have periods of positivity in between bouts of negative thoughts. The negative thoughts are a symptom of the problem, they do not define the individual and it is possible to overcome this uncomfortable problem.

The path to breaking free from negative thinking is to work on becoming more self-aware and paying attention to what is going on within. By becoming inquisitive about the thoughts we are having we can explore them with a mindful curiosity instead of a default emotional reaction, over time we can train ourselves not to be afraid of looking closer at our thoughts and work on removing the power they have held over us.

There are some excellent videos, books and podcasts (some of which can be found in the Resources section at the end of this book) that can help you to overcome negative thought patterns; therapy can also be beneficial.

⇨ Can anxiety affect my memory?

An anxiety disorder can affect memory, usually when the stress response has been triggered and we have perceived that there is some kind of threat or danger.

During the times when we can experience memory problems we might be worrying excessively or stuck in a loop of negative thoughts that won't leave us alone. These stressful periods cause us to focus almost exclusively on the troubling thoughts which can result in us having difficulty accessing essential memories as we enter a tunnel-vision-like state.

The working memory is an important brain function which allows us to keep track of what we are doing – it is also that part that is most affected during a stress response. The working memory is a built-in reminder system of what we need to do, and if you are caught up in challenging thoughts you may find yourself forgetting where you've left your car keys or phone, or you might fail to carry out a task you had promised to complete. To an outside observer you may appear absent minded, but this isn't the case. Instead, anxiety is taking up so much of your mental bandwidth that there is very little room left for you to be able to focus on anything else.

⇨ Can anxiety lead to addiction?

There is no doubt that alcohol, drugs and most other addictive behaviours can make anxiety much worse and that strong cravings for our addiction of choice have the hallmarks of an anxiety attack.

People who experience heightened anxiety can find it difficult to cope with the constant thoughts and non-stop worries and may use addictive behaviour as a method of self-medicating and feeling as though they have a level of control.

Additionally, many people have a hard-wired fear of feeling any type of uncomfortable feelings, particularly if they were brought up in a household where they were given the message that feelings like anger and sadness were bad or unsafe and should not be expressed. When this is the case there is often a strong subconscious desire to avoid these feelings at any cost.

The reality is that any kind of addictive behaviour has negative consequences and none of them will get rid of anxiety. Alcohol, drugs and other so-called coping mechanisms may hit the pause button for a short period of time, but the anxiety is always waiting to return and often comes back far worse than it was before.

Addictions don't have to involve substances like alcohol and drugs; many people develop unhealthy coping mechanisms with activities that may appear healthy or normal to an outsider. But when the behaviour has control over someone, it is not healthy and it is important to identify whether an otherwise healthy pastime has become something more sinister.

When people find themselves obsessing over a behaviour and thinking about it most of the time then there is a chance it has become an addiction. If the behaviour is causing negative consequences yet someone is still unable to stop it, then it is a sure sign they need to get curious about what is happening and take steps towards change.

The easiest way to assess whether a behaviour has become an addiction is to ask yourself whether you are in control of it, or whether it is in control of you. If your answer is the latter, then the likelihood is that it has become addictive and you need to take steps to break free.

Here are some of the most common addictions people with anxiety use as a coping mechanism.

- Alcohol: Alcohol is an addictive substance that provides a short-term relief from anxious feelings. However, it has been shown to elevate anxiety once the effects have worn off and once someone has become addicted to drinking they will generally experience anxious thoughts about their inability to control their behaviour.

- Drugs: Aside from the fact that most drugs are illegal, they are also usually highly addictive and can play havoc with anxiety, especially as the effects begin to wear off. Depending on the drug involved there are also wide ranging side effects and risks. If you are concerned about a problem with drug abuse, please contact your local narcotics anonymous for support.

- Work: It can be all too easy to fall into the trap of work addiction, especially as it makes people feel as though they are doing their best to generate an income, feel recognition and further their career. When the work/life balance becomes negatively impacted and a career is taking preference over friends, family and hobbies it is likely time to look closer at the reasons behind the need to spend so much time wrapped up in work.

- Love and sex: A sense of inadequacy (also known as toxic shame) exists at the root of most addictive behaviour. The feeling of being loved and wanted by another person is one of the most powerful forces against feeling not good enough, which is why millions of people around the world become addicted to seeking love by acting out through affairs, one night stands, illicit encounters and seeking connection outside a relationship.

- Exercise: Because exercise generates a release of endorphins and dopamine it can give people a 'high' that brings a sense of euphoria. This chemical release can be addictive and addicts can become dependent on the feeling. Although exercise in moderation is beneficial, when someone has developed an addiction it can become obsessive and have damaging effects.

- *Food*: We all need to eat in order to stay alive but when our nutrition plans become an obsession defined by overeating it is usually an addiction. Many people who develop a problem with food will eat foods that are high in calories, sugar and fat, they will often do it in secret to experience a 'high' from the feel good reactions triggered by the reward centre in the brain. This leaves people with a strong desire to repeat the behaviour and they can experience cravings and withdrawal symptoms if they try and stop.

- *Smoking and vaping*: As with the other addictions, smoking and vaping activate the reward centre in the brain and deliver a fast feel-good hit. Because the reaction is so quick, the withdrawal is equally swift and this can cause people to chain smoke or vape as they enter a continual cycle of craving followed by reward.

While anxiety does not specifically cause addiction, it is common for people with an anxiety disorder to use these kinds of mechanisms to cope. If you are concerned you may have developed an addiction please ensure you seek out the appropriate support as soon as possible.

If you believe you have a problem with alcohol I recommend reading my book *How to Quit Alcohol in 50 Days* (Sheldon Press, 2020).

Are people with anxiety more likely to engage in risky behaviour?

People who engage in risky behaviour can make choices that cause them to put themselves or others at risk. Most types of risky behaviour come with some level of negative consequences and almost all of them will leave people feeling a sense of guilt or shame at some point after the event.

There is no hard evidence that shows that people with an anxiety disorder engage in risky behaviour. However some studies have shown that people with social anxiety are more likely to use drugs or alcohol to excess.

5 common types of risky behaviour

1. drink driving or reckless driving
2. unprotected sex
3. drug or alcohol abuse
4. violence or anger towards others
5. other types of illegal activities.

People are more likely to engage in risky behaviour when they have been drinking alcohol or taking drugs as their inhibitions will have been lowered, meaning they are far less in control of themselves and the choices they make. They will commonly act in ways that are not in line with their values and may find that they end up in trouble or put themselves in danger through their behaviour while intoxicated.

Given that people with anxiety may be more predisposed to addictive substances or behaviours due to the way in which they suppress anxious feelings, it follows that risky behaviour is more likely in someone who is struggling with worries and fears.

Risky behaviour can deliver a similar 'high' to drugs or alcohol through the release of endorphins and dopamine can become as addictive as the substances themselves.

What is the best way of managing difficult emotions?

Jai says: 'When I was suffering with anxiety I was plagued by uncomfortable thoughts, difficult feelings and strong emotions. I felt as though they were holding me captive and did all I could to try and break free and avoid them, this usually meant opening a bottle of wine to numb them.

'I eventually realized that numbing the anxious feelings was not getting rid of them, in fact they were returning stronger than before. I learned that when I tried to resist anxious feelings and emotions they would expand and persist, there was no way of erasing them, and they usually got worse.

'I finally realized that I needed to develop a new level of self-awareness so I could begin to understand exactly how I was feeling. Over the years I had become so emotionally disconnected I didn't even know how I felt, I just knew I didn't like the feeling.

'I started by using an "emotion wheel" which enabled me to get really clear on how I was feeling at any given time. I labelled every emotion and made this a new healthy habit which enabled me to understand myself far better.

'Once I had worked out what feeling or emotion was with me, I resisted any urge to shut it down, either with substances or other types of unhelpful or addictive behaviours. I needed to learn how to feel and express what was within me.

'I had become afraid of my own emotions so I reframed my thinking and formed new beliefs that there was no such thing as bad or negative feelings because they were with me for a reason and more than likely trying to act as a signpost to help me understand what I needed.

'The more I paid attention to my feelings and emotions rather than trying to push them away, the more comfortable I became with them. Previously I believed I either felt happy or sad or calm or angry, everything was black and white and I had to hide from anything other than a positive feeling.

'As I expanded my emotional toolbox I learned that I could work out exactly what I needed when an uncomfortable emotion arose within me, the following process will help you do the same.'

Process for meeting your own needs

Step 1: Identify the emotion or feeling that is with you at the moment. It may feel like anger or sadness, but when you dig deeper or use an emotion wheel you will likely be able to get much more specific. I often firmly believed I was angry but would end up working out that the real feeling was one of being unheard, unloved or rejected.

Step 2: Once you have identified the specific emotion that you are holding, try to embrace it and avoid any attempts to push it away. The feelings always pass, allow it to be with you and try to listen to what it is saying.

Step 3: What is the opposite of the emotion you are feeling? This is what you will need to do in order to meet your needs, this is where your emotion is signposting you. In my example of feeling unheard, the opposite would be feeling listened to and connected to others.

Step 4: Work out where you can get the opposite of the emotion you are feeling. When I felt unheard and realized that I needed to be listened to and connected to others I would reach out to a close friend and might arrange to meet them for a chat over coffee, this would give me exactly what I needed.

Managing difficult emotions and feelings

You may find some of the following to be extremely helpful in overcoming anxiety and eliminating a negative mood and mindset.

- *Writing in a journal*: If you use a journal daily, you can track your mood and explore any feelings or emotions that have arisen within you. A journal can help you to get thoughts out of your head and on to paper, taking away much of their power and allowing you some perspective on your fears and worries.

- *Meditation and visualization techniques*: Meditation apps can play a big role in helping you reduce your anxiety and manage your emotions: try to fit in two short practices each day. Sitting with your eyes closed, visualizing difficult emotions as passing clouds and watching them until they shrunk away into the distance is an excellent way of allowing them to pass without trying to force anything. See the Resources section at the end of this book for some suggestions.

- *The 5-4-3-2-1 technique*: This technique involves noticing and naming five things that you can see, four things you can touch, three things that you can hear, two things that you can smell and one thing that you can taste. You can also use this technique when anxious feelings are building to allow you to get back in control.

- *Vigorous exercise*: Vigorous exercise – if you're physically capable of it – is a great way to eliminate difficult feelings quickly. This also helps when cravings strike to try and draw us back to addictive patterns of behaviour. Try 25 jumping jacks in your back garden and notice how the feelings begin to fade, if they haven't completely disappeared try another twenty five and you will probably have seen the last of them.

- Therapy: One-to-one and group therapy can play a big part in helping you reconnect with your feelings and emotions while learning to understand and accept your anxiety.

Anxiety tip

When you experience a negative thought that causes uncomfortable feelings, try to visualize it as though you have just put your hand on a hot stove. By dwelling on the thought you are keeping your hand on the stove and inflicting more pain on yourself. Instead, when you notice the feelings immediately turn to what brings you joy in order to step away from the stove and allow happiness to flow in.

The physical cost of anxiety

It can be easy to believe that because anxiety is a mental health condition it only impacts people in their minds, this is not the case. In this part of the book we explore how anxiety can impact people on a physical level and how you can avoid the problems that can easily arise when we fail to pay attention to the far reaching damage that an anxiety disorder can cause.

What is the link between anxiety and the human body?

Healthy anxiety is a perfectly normal feeling that has the purpose of alerting us that we may be exposed to danger or some kind of threat. The warning signals arrive in the shape of an increased heart rate and faster breathing which can help us become more focused to handle a difficult situation.

You might feel anxiety before an important job interview, public speaking or a driving test – this is perfectly normal.

When anxiety becomes a problem the symptoms can cause more extreme effects on the body. If left unmanaged these can worsen over time and develop into debilitating anxiety attacks, constant negative thinking and physical health problems.

The main effects of anxiety on the body

- **Breathing problems**: Faster breathing is a normal part of an anxious response, but when the breath becomes shallow and the rate of breathing is more rapid it is a sign of a problem that can lead to an anxiety attack.

- **Increased heart rate**: People with an anxiety disorder often describe the feeling of a pounding heart during times of increased stress or an anxiety attack. The intensity and pace increases with the level of anxiety and this can lead to overwhelming feelings of being out of control.

- **Stomach problems**: Anxiety has a direct impact on the stomach and can cause pains, upset and diarrhea.

- **Aching muscles**: Heightened anxiety can cause muscle aches and pains that are largely unexplained but likely to be related to the reduced flow of blood to the muscles during increased stress and anxiety attacks.

- **Headaches and migraines**: It is common for anxiety sufferers to experience headaches often due to the constant worries and negative thoughts.

Over the longer term the physical impact of stress hormone release and extreme anxiety can have more serious consequences including:

- problems with the immune system making people more prone to illness

- digestion problems and disorders

- insomnia and trouble getting to sleep

- feeling irritable and moody most of the time

- increased risk of coronary disease and heart problems.

It is important to pay attention to what is happening in your own experience. Take the time to document the symptoms you have, along with their frequency and strength, in your journal. This will allow you to gather important data and track any patterns so you can take steps to address the problems.

Can anxiety weaken my immune system?

Our immune system is a crucial element of our wellbeing as it ensures that we remain protected against illnesses. It acts as a powerful defence against bacteria and germs and will destroy them to prevent us becoming sick. When the immune system is not functioning correctly, or if it has been weakened, it can be much less effective when it comes to warding off potential sources of illness.

When we experience anxious reactions and feelings for long periods of time, it can cause problems with the immune system. Stressful responses create a release of cortisol, a stress hormone, which in small doses is not harmful but with prolonged periods of anxiety it can suppress bodily functions that help the immune system function properly and weaken the protection we have against harmful bacteria and germs.

There is limited evidence about the exact impact of anxiety on the immune system, but the research that has been carried out shows a clear link between anxious feelings and a weakening in the body's natural defences.

Does anxiety increase blood pressure?

During an anxiety attack, or times when we are experiencing heightened anxiety, it is common for our blood pressure to increase, before returning to normal after the episode has passed. The more frequently we experience anxiety, the more often we will encounter fluctuations in our blood pressure.

While anxiety alone does not cause long-lasting high blood pressure, there is a risk that continual fluctuations over a long period of time due to stress can cause damage to the heart, kidneys and blood vessels which can lead to serious problems related to heightened blood pressure. The risk of physical consequences is low, but the message is clear – stress can be bad for your health and the more you can do to practise healthy levels of anxiety, the better.

➡️ Does anxiety increase the risk of cancer?

There is no evidence that anxiety or increased stress can cause cancer, however it is common for people with cancer to experience heightened stress and anxiety.

While anxiety may not be a direct cause of cancer, there is no doubt that people who suffer anxiety may use unhealthy coping mechanisms such as:

- smoking or vaping
- drinking too much alcohol
- poor nutrition choices
- lack of exercise
- failing to relax or enjoy downtime
- over-working.

All of these unhealthy behaviours can increase the risk of developing cancer, so it is important to ensure that healthy ways of treating the symptoms of anxiety are found.

Can anxiety cause hair loss?

Although it is rare, in some cases anxiety can lead to hair loss. While an anxiety disorder itself does not specifically cause hair loss, the extreme stress that arises as a result of an anxiety disorder can.

Some people experience clumps of hair falling out due to a condition known as *alopecia areata* and others may notice thinning hair due to stress causing less follicles to produce healthy hair, this is known as *telogen effluvium*.

Hair loss can be an incredibly challenging symptom to deal with, especially as most sufferers feel even more stressed when they notice the problem.

You can help reduce the chances of hair loss by ensuring your hair is receiving the essential nutrients required to remain healthy. When we are under increased stress our body can use these crucial nutrients to deal with the immediate response and take them away from the hair.

There are numerous hair treatments that can help ensure you get the right nutrients and it is worth speaking to a specialist if you would like to get advice. Maintaining a healthy lifestyle with regular exercise and a nutritious diet will also help maintain healthy hair follicles.

Is anxiety impacted by my weight?

The chances of developing an anxiety disorder are not increased if someone is overweight or obese. However, research has shown that people with anxiety problems can subsequently experience issues with their weight.*

---

* https://www.ncbi.nlm.nih.gov/pmc/articles/PMC2727271/

Studies show that people suffering from an anxiety disorder are more likely to gain weight over time than people with normal anxiety levels. Anxiety can cause people to isolate themselves and this increases the chances of them avoiding healthy activities such as exercising and eating well. These lifestyle choices are a major factor in preventing weight gain.

Although it can feel hard, it is important for people who suffer with anxiety to create a routine that ensures they are providing themselves with a healthy dose of activity. Exercise is one of the best antidotes for anxiety due to it providing a boost of dopamine and serotonin, the feel-good chemicals that are released during fitness that can significantly reduce anxious feelings.

Is anxiety linked to gut health?

The primary function of our gut is to help us swallow and digest food, but there is a lesser known link between our stomach and our brain. The human digestive system contains millions of tiny nerve cells that communicate directly with the brain. While their main role is to regulate and manage stomach activity, scientists have discovered that they also play a part when it comes to balancing mood and emotion.

If you have ever had a 'gut feeling' about something, you will have already experienced the power of this incredible system which has led to the area of the stomach called the enteric nervous system becoming known as the second brain. The effects of this system are felt strongest during bouts of stomach problems, such as irritable bowel syndrome where people often feel significant shifts in their mood and anxiety.

Problems in the stomach, gut and digestive system do appear to be able to increase anxiety, however it is an area of science where new discoveries and breakthroughs are being made and currently not enough is known to be certain about the exact link between the two.

Anyone who is experiencing increased anxiety should pay attention to their gut health. Choosing a diet that is high in collagen, fibre and omega-3 fatty acids will help minimize the risk of stomach problems and the potential anxiety that might follow.

The best foods to maintain a healthy gut

For omega-3 fatty acids:

- fatty fish such as salmon, herring and mackerel

- anchovies

- walnuts

- chia seeds

- fortified foods, such as yoghurt, juice, milk and soy drinks.

For fibre:

- wholegrain foods, such as pasta, cereals and bread

- fruit, including oranges, berries and melon

- vegetables, such as broccoli and carrots

- seeds and beans

- potatoes with skin on.

To boost collagen:

- bone broth

- egg whites

- fish and shellfish

- tropical and citrus fruits

- chicken, especially neck and cartilage.

How many people die because of anxiety?

While an anxiety attack can feel totally overwhelming and people can feel as though they are having a heart attack or unable to breathe, it cannot directly bring about fatal consequences. It is, however, true that anxiety disorders can contribute to some longer-term health problems.

There are numerous factors to consider, but the fact is that those people who make healthy lifestyle choices are significantly less at risk of developing cancer, heart disease or having a stroke.

Simple lifestyle changes including a balanced diet, regular exercise and reduced stress will serve to minimize anxiety and lead to improved health and wellbeing. It is worth creating a plan to incorporate each of these areas into your life.

- Diet: Consider the 80/20 – try and eat healthy foods 80 per cent of the time and allow 20 per cent for treats. Plan your meals in advance as this will save you time and money as well as enabling you to avoid getting caught out with no evening meal and heading to the takeaway.

- Exercise: Think about what exercise you enjoy and work out how you can do more of it. This might be swimming, cycling, pilates or running, for example. Are there any local fitness clubs you can join? If so, can you make a commitment to take part two or three times a week?

- Stress: Work out which areas of your life are bringing you stress and consider how you can minimize them. If you struggle keeping on top of housework because you are caught up with looking after the kids and working, then maybe it is time to bring in some outside help.

Does the nervous system control anxiety?

Anxiety is a response triggered by the release of stress hormones when the fight, flight or freeze reaction is activated. This is a perfectly natural response that is built into humans to help them survive when they are faced with a threat or danger, but those with anxiety disorders will experience an uncomfortable reaction when no real danger is present.

All humans have a parasympathetic nervous system and a sympathetic nervous system. One acts like a brake pedal on anxiety (parasympathetic) and enables us to feel calm, relaxed and less anxious, while the other behaves like an anxiety accelerator (sympathetic) by heightening the sense of fear and worry.

Because the nervous system is in the driving seat of anxiety it might be useful to understand how to activate the parasympathetic nervous system in order to trigger the body's relaxation response.

 ## 10 tips for activating your parasympathetic nervous system

 1 Anxiety can cause a Try vigorous exercise such as running, cycling or swimming.

 2 Take a deep breath in then close your mouth and pinch your nostrils as you try and breathe out: this increases pressure in your chest and stimulates the parasympathetic nervous system.

3 Vigorously shake your hands and feet – a great way to quickly release tension and nervous energy.

4 Gargle with water – as you activate the muscles at the back of your throat you will also trigger the parasympathetic nervous system.

 5 Laugh intentionally – even if you have to fake it, the process of laughing stimulates the parasympathetic nervous system and will help you feel calm and relaxed.

 6 Do what you know what brings you joy (hobbies, activities).

 7 Deep rhythmic breathing exercises – try breathing deeply from the diaphragm with your eyes closed for several minutes to experience the most powerful results.

 8 Meditation and mindfulness practice provide a gateway to feeling more in control and at peace quickly.

 9 Yoga, pilates or tai chi – all have a calming effect and with regular practice we can access a new level of relaxation.

➡️ 10 physical symptoms you may not have known were caused by anxiety

Some physical symptoms of anxiety are well known, but you may have experienced others that you didn't realize were occurring as a result of heightened anxious feelings.

 1 *Tingling skin and numbness:* Anxiety can cause a tingling sensation or numbness almost anywhere on the body; most commonly it is felt in the hands and fingers or on the face, arms, legs or feet.

2 *Teeth grinding:* Anxiety can cause people to clench their jaw and grind their teeth, known as bruxism. Although it can happen while awake, it is more common to experience this while sleeping, over time it can lead to jaw and facial pain.

Yawning: During a heightened period of anxiety or a panic attack, your body may feel that it isn't getting enough oxygen, as a result you may find yourself yawning more.

Needing the toilet: When we feel anxious our body moves into a protective state and does all it can to keep us safe from the perceived threat (of course, with an anxiety disorder the threat is rarely real). Part of the response involves the body moving blood away from any areas where it is not needed, which can cause a churning sensation in the stomach. Some people experience the need to use the toilet, and this is the body attempting to get rid of any unnecessary weight that could slow it down during the fight, flight or freeze response.

 Lump in the throat: Anxiety can cause a symptom called *globus hystericus* which causes a sensation best described as a tightness in the throat. Some people report difficulty swallowing or feel a lump in their throat.

Blurry vision: When we perceive a threat, the fight, flight or freeze response will tune us into a heightened state of protection. Our pupils will become dilated to allow more light in so we can see as clearly as possible during a dangerous situation. For some people, the extra light can cause blurred vision.

 Acne and skin problems: The production of increased stress hormones can cause the skin to produce more oil than is needed, which in turn can cause spots and acne. Skin problems can also be caused by increased sweating during anxious episodes which can clog pores and cause breakouts of spots and acne.

Hiccups: Caused by involuntary spasms in the diaphragm, hiccups are usually linked to digestion problems. However, mental or emotional distress has been proven to be another cause.

 Ringing in the ears: Also known as tinnitus, some people experience ringing, buzzing or humming sounds when they encounter heightened periods of anxiety.

 Detachment from reality: Also known as derealization, anxious people can feel disconnected from the world as though they are watching things happen from the outside and looking in or have a sense of being in a dream-like state.

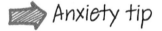 ## Anxiety tip

What small daily goals can you set for yourself? Try to be consistent by setting targets that are achievable. Exercise is one of the best ways to reduce anxiety – how about a short morning walk, jog or cycle ride?

Anxiety and relationships

In some cases anxiety can prove to be devastating for relationships, especially the most intimate ones. In this section of the book we will explore how you can learn to thrive in your most important relationships by no longer allowing anxiety to interfere with them.

How does anxiety affect relationships?

Anxiety can have a significant effect on relationships, whether with friends, family or a partner – the impact can be far reaching. Those who live with people who have anxiety disorders may feel as though they are walking on eggshells and might struggle to know what to do for the best.

If you have anxiety, you might feel emotionally detached from your most important relationships as much of your mental bandwidth is being used to focus on your anxious worries and concerns. Perhaps your partner, friends and family feel that you are not fully present, interested or engaged.

Anxious people tend to spend a lot of time talking about their worries in an effort to obtain reassurance. Although they don't mean it to be, this can be draining for the people around them on whom they are relying for advice, comfort and support.

It's very hard to find joy when you're stuck in a cycle of worry, and this can have an impact on meaningful relationships.

Poppy has a suggestion: 'I got so fed up of feeling trapped and grumpy. I started to try and find a more playful mood when I was with my partner, making myself laugh and have fun with her, even if it meant faking it a bit. It helped to diminish my own feelings of anxiety a bit, and I felt more present in the relationship.'

⮕ Do people with anxiety struggle to form relationships?

If you have social anxiety, you might try to avoid situations where you meet new people, which in turn reduces your chances of connecting with someone you may go on to form a relationship with.

If you're experiencing generalized anxiety disorder, you might enjoy social events and be able to form relationships, but you could also find yourself hiding your anxiety until you feel comfortable enough with another person to allow it to come out into the light.

Anxiety doesn't need to hold you back from forming meaningful relationships and connections with others, and when you equip yourself with the right tools and support you will quickly build the confidence to enable yourself to face the fear and do it anyway.

Almost always our anxious thoughts do not match the real-world outcome. We might fear attending a party, for example, and convince ourselves we will have a bad time and that nobody will talk to us. Once we experience the reality by heading out and having a good time we become more confident, which in turn causes us to form new beliefs that do not limit us from any social opportunities that may arise.

For many people it can take time to begin facing the fears associated with social events and it is important to take baby steps and move forward at a pace that feels right for you. Instead of throwing yourself head first into the next party there are plenty of other ways you can meet people and form new and meaningful relationships.

You might find it easier to slowly build your social circle with people who you feel comfortable around and there is nothing wrong with picking and choosing the social events you attend based on what feels right for you.

If you want to work on improving your social life and form new relationships, it is worth having a strategy to help yourself grow and develop this aspect of your life. If you need help building confidence and managing the challenging feelings that can come with social interactions it may be worth investing in a few sessions of cognitive behavioural therapy (CBT) or confidence coaching.

Alternative ways to connect with new people and form new relationships

- Connect in online groups – Facebook has thousands of private groups based around specific topics and interests.

- Check out meet-up websites – meet-up websites list local groups and clubs based on interests and location.

- Take up a class so you can learn something new and meet people who share the same passions and interests.

- Explore what local community events take place in your area and attend those that interest you.

- Ask your close friends to introduce you to their friends that you haven't met yet.

- Consider a career that allows you to connect and interact with new people.

- Try online dating – there are countless apps and websites that allow you to connect with new people who are looking for love.

➤ Will anxiety make me a bad parent?

Anxiety sufferers can spend large amounts of time trapped in a cycle of worry and negative thinking, at times this can cause them to seem distant and unable to be fully present for the people around them, including their children.

As parents it is important to be emotionally available for our children. They crave our attention and when an anxiety disorder is taking this away by blocking our ability to be fully connected, it can have long-lasting negative effects that can surface when our kids move into adulthood.

While having anxiety does not make someone a bad parent, it can cause them to be less connected and emotionally available due to the overwhelming amount of their headspace that is being engulfed by anxious thoughts.

The good news is that when we bring a conscious awareness to anxious thoughts and feelings, and combine this with the tools and techniques outlined in this book, it becomes possible to reclaim control in order that we can focus fully on being the best parent we can possibly be.

➤ Can anxiety affect my sex life?

The simple answer is yes, very much so. Our sex lives can be negatively impacted by anxiety in several different ways. Sex is one of the best ways of feeling connected to our partner. When anxiety starts affecting our ability to engage in physical intimacy, it can have a profound impact on our relationship.

The most common behaviour traits in anxiety sufferers are the polar opposite of each other: sex avoidance and sex addiction.

Sex avoidance

Many people with an anxiety disorder can become sex averse and avoid physical intimacy wherever possible. This can be through fears around performance, body image or being rejected. It can seem easier to avoid sex altogether rather than pushing through the difficult feelings and emotions associated with such intense connection.

Avoiding sex can also be related to past trauma, especially when there has been a history of sexual abuse. People can also become sex averse due to physical symptoms of an anxiety disorder and end up finding themselves in a challenging cycle of behaviour where they desperately long for physical connection but feel unable to engage.

Avoidance may be as a result of tiredness, migraines, stomach problems or any number of other physical symptoms related to an anxiety disorder.

Sex addiction

Sex is an important expression of love, and this is especially the case for people who have an overwhelming need for physical intimacy. This is usually a need born out of a desire to feel reassured that they are 'enough' while at the same time making them feel wanted and needed, even when this level of connection feels impossible with their partner.

For some the need for sex is so great that they choose to meet it with different or alternative partners. Some may use sex workers or engage in one-night stands to satisfy their desire. However the reality is that the underlying need is rarely met and people often feel worse after this type of encounter, with many experiencing lingering issues around self-worth and esteem.

Sex, along with other types of addiction can also be a method of blotting out the discomfort caused by anxiety. It can provide a short period of respite from the racing thoughts and constant worries, but when engaging in casual sex it can often cause more worrying, especially if we are breaching the trust of our partner and end up having to keep secrets.

Awareness is the key to overcoming challenges around sex and anxiety, when you become able to identify the problem and get really clear about how it is impacting your life you can begin to take positive steps towards change.

Can my partner help me eliminate anxiety?

Mika says: 'I spent much of my life in a relationship where my anxiety drove me to become co-dependent on my wife. I expected her to solve my problems or second guess how I felt and I would become upset if I didn't feel she was meeting my needs. It took me lots of therapy, and a much deeper understanding of what was causing my anxiety, to realize that only one person is responsible for looking after me: *me*.'

Mika is right. While your partner can be part of your support network and will likely be a huge help on your journey to overcoming anxiety, it is not their responsibility to fix the problem and if you find yourself placing unrealistic expectations on them, take a step back and remind yourself that only you have the power to manage your anxiety, no matter how much you hope or expect other people to do it for you.

Mika adds: 'I had a breakthrough when I realized the expectations I had been placing on my wife were unrealistic, and my constant need for reassurance was causing problems in our relationship. I took ownership of my behaviour and worked hard to take personal responsibility for my anxiety disorder.'

One way to help to tackle your anxiety is to try and work on building your emotional intimacy with your partner. It starts with you, and it will mean taking a leap of faith by showing your inside on the outside. When we let our partners see into us, things begin to change and we cultivate a whole new level of connection and trust.

Are people with anxiety more likely to end up alone?

Millions of people who suffer with anxiety are in a relationship – having a disorder does not mean you are destined to a lifetime of being alone. That said, it is important to take steps to work on the symptoms of anxiety so as to ensure it doesn't have a negative impact on your relationships.

Living with a partner who has an anxiety disorder can be a challenge. If you can take the time to become vulnerable and open about the challenges you are facing you will likely find that your partner will want to work with you and help you overcome the difficulties you are encountering.

Learning to open up and become truly authentic can feel difficult, but it can also be hugely liberating and allow you to take a big step forward along the path to healing and finding peace. Start by naming and labelling your feelings and emotions and begin to openly share them with your partner so you can talk about them and experience a deeper level of communication and connection.

➡ Will anxiety cause problems if I want to become a parent?

Several studies have shown that stress and anxiety can affect fertility and reduce the chances of conceiving. The stress hormones that are released when we are anxious can have a negative impact on the reproductive system which can make it harder if we want to try for a baby.

Anxiety can cause further problems with conception by causing problems with hormone levels and menstrual cycles in women. In men it can have a negative effect on the libido and sperm count.

On the other hand, countless babies are born to parents who live in areas of conflict, war zones or in stressful environments, so it is not by any means inevitable that anxiety impacts fertility, but it's a good idea to make good choices about your lifestyle wherever you can, so as to mitigate any effects of anxiety.

There is some evidence that cortisol – the stress hormone – can be passed from mother to unborn baby but the best mitigation against your anxiety having an effect on your child in or ex-utero is to be engaged with your anxiety, take steps where you can to manage it, and to nurture and support your child at every stage.

If you are planning on having children, minimising the impact of your anxiety on them might be a strong motivation for you to start taking positive steps towards managing it.

➡ 5 tips for improving the chances of conceiving

 Track your menstrual cycle: By using a diary or an app you can work out when you might be ovulating and know when you stand the best chances of becoming pregnant.

2 | *Stay healthy:* By maintaining a healthy lifestyle rich in nutrients and exercise you will be giving yourself the best chances of conceiving. However, be mindful that overdoing exercise can interfere with ovulation so try and maintain a sensible balance.

3 | *Stop smoking:* The chemicals in cigarettes and vapes can accelerate how quickly women lose their eggs which creates a smaller window of opportunity when it comes to getting pregnant. Even second-hand smoke can cause problems and it is important to eliminate tobacco products.

4 | *Cut out alcohol:* Just one or two drinks a day can significantly reduce the chances of getting pregnant, in order to set yourself up for success it is recommended that you stop drinking when you are trying to conceive.

5 | *Don't be afraid to ask for help:* If you have been trying to conceive for over six months without success, it might be time to reach out for help. There are count-less fertility specialists who will be able to offer expert assistance and advice.

Anxiety tip

How could you get more involved in your local community and enable yourself to meet new people in a way that you enjoy and feel comfortable with? Come up with three different options and choose which one you would like to try.

Anxiety at work

Many people with anxiety encounter significant problems in the workplace. It can be an area of our lives where we can easily feel overwhelmed and out of control. Use this section to learn exactly how to flourish in your career by claiming back the power over an anxiety disorder.

🖎 Can anxiety hold me back in my career?

It is true that anxiety in the workplace has the potential to cause problems. Around one in seven people have said they have experienced mental health problems at work* – you could indeed describe it as an epidemic. As modern workplaces place ever-increasing demands on staff, it can be easy to allow negative thoughts and unhelpful worries to take over, but there's no need for anxiety to impact or disrupt your career. Indeed, many employers have woken up to the problem and take steps to ensure the mental wellbeing of their staff is made a priority.

But while increased stress is often part of working life, when it becomes debilitating it is important to take action to look after yourself. An anxiety disorder shouldn't hold you back in your career. If you feel your anxiety has caused you to be unfairly treated – overlooked for promotion, for example – this behaviour is discrimination. It is illegal, and if you feel this might apply

---

* https://www.mentalhealth.org.uk/statistics/mental-health-statistics-mental-health-work

to you it is important to speak up about it and take steps to have your voice heard.

🡆 10 tips to minimize anxiety at work

1 **Know when to ask for help:** It can seem all too easy to be a martyr even when things feel really tough. This is a surefire way to increase your anxieties and worries. Don't be afraid to ask for help, especially when you are finding yourself struggling.

2 **Don't fight your anxiety:** Anxiety is a perfectly natural response to stress and workplaces can create the perfect storm when it comes to anxious feelings. Instead of trying to wrestle with anxious thoughts or attempting to push them away, try and make time and space for them while you are at work. This might mean taking a short break to meditate, keeping a journal by your desk or talking your feelings through with a supportive colleague.

3 **Be authentic and honest:** Many people with anxiety have a strong need to please others. This includes our employers. There is nothing wrong with being ambitious, but it is important to be careful not to over promise or set unrealistic expectations that may come back to bite you. Try to practise being radically honest and authentic, especially in the workplace and it will help you minimize unwanted worries and fears.

4 **Avoid drama:** Workplaces are full of drama, with gossip and idle chat being the staple diet of many people. This kind of toxicity can cause you to become embroiled in unhealthy and negative situations that are almost guaranteed to induce anxiety. Stay alert and notice when you are being pulled into a drama situation and when you spot it, walk away.

5 *Practise mindfulness:* It is easy for worries and negative thoughts to become overwhelming and this can impact our productivity in the workplace. By practising mindfulness and working on being fully present in the moment, we can train ourselves to stay focused and reduce the impact of unwanted thoughts.

6 *Face your fears:* Maybe you have an upcoming presentation and you are anxious about delivering it in front of your colleagues or potential new clients. The worst thing you can do is give into your anxiety and allow it to have control over you. Instead take the time to find resources and support that will help you become able to face your fears and overcome them. This will help you reclaim some of the power anxiety has likely taken away from you.

7 *Get rational:* Our minds are the masters of making up stories and when we don't have all the facts they will often fill in the blanks and beat us up with negative self-talk, criticisms and judgements. It isn't always sensible to trust the stories we tell ourselves, and by using a journal and writing down your thoughts you can become objective about your inner dialogue and will find that you are able to get a far more rational perspective on things.

8 *Know when you need a break:* Many people use work as a coping mechanism and spend vast amounts of time immersed in their careers. It is a great way to avoid negative thoughts and feelings as it keeps them constantly busy and on the go. Work, just like drugs and alcohol, can become an addiction if we allow it. Take the time to monitor the balance between your work and home life, know when it is time to fully switch off from your career and most importantly allow yourself to have regular breaks so you can relax and decompress.

9 *Have a life away from work:* As well as making time for yourself away from your career, it is important that your job does not define you as a person. Use a piece of paper and answer these questions: *Who am I really, without my career, my possessions, my status and my money? Who is the person behind it all? What do they look like?*

Rubina struggled to answer this question and says 'Exploring this question opened my eyes to the importance of engaging in hobbies and activities that brought me real joy. I worked out that in my case painting, running and writing are my passions but I had allowed them to take a backseat while I was busy attempting to please others in a career I wasn't enjoying. I was using unhelpful coping mechanisms that were actually making my anxiety worse.'

10 *Reach out:* If you are finding being in your workplace to be a challenge, don't be afraid to speak to a manager or supervisor. Many firms have dedicated occupational health specialists and understand the importance of maintaining positive mental health among their staff. Don't allow shame to hold you back from reaching out for help. There is no shame in anxiety and you will very likely make your own life significantly better by speaking up when you need to do so.

What is performance anxiety?

Workplace performance anxiety is more commonly known as stage-fright and relates to the fear of a specific task, often involving a group of people. This might be speaking publicly, hosting a meeting or running a training session, for example. Performance anxiety tends to arise when we are faced with a situation that puts us outside of our comfort zone.

Performance anxiety usually begins with negative thoughts about the specific event which expand into catastrophic scenarios about how wrong it might go.

Suheil says: 'I used to have to deliver a monthly presentation when I worked as a marketing director for a legal firm. I would spend most of the month worrying about it and eventually I allowed the anxiety to win and asked one of the partners to deliver the presentation on my behalf. I wish I hadn't now – I realized later that the best way to have got over fear would be to understand that the worst case scenarios were unlikely to be as catastrophic as the ones in my head.'

5 tips to help overcome performance anxiety

1. **Speak about topics you really care about:** If you aren't fully invested in your subject matter then doubts will likely creep in and you won't be truly motivated. If you don't feel totally motivated ask yourself why and listen carefully to your answers.

2. **Take the time to prepare:** Practise and refine your talk or presentation. Make sure you have prepared it, rehearsed it and planned how you will deliver it – even if it means you practise so much that you know the talk off by heart.

3. **Regulate your nervous system:** Before starting, try to find somewhere private where you can vigorously shake your hands and feet to ensure your nervous system doesn't take over. Some people find that putting headphones in before a live event and listening to a couple of songs makes them feel really motivated and energized.

4 Get familiar with your surroundings: If it is possible to spend some time in the room or on the stage ahead of the event, then take a chance to simply walk around it and sit in stillness so it doesn't feel alien when the time comes to walk on and deliver your talk.

5 Break the ice: One of the best methods of feeling calmer when you are presenting is to get some early audience interaction. Make eye contact, treat them like your friends and ask for a show of hands or a response to a question early on.

Are people with anxiety less employable?

Anxiety in the workplace can present some challenges to those of us who experience it, and yes, we need to take individual responsibility for our own wellbeing. However, it is the responsibility of our employers to recognize these challenges, too, and to take steps to minimize stress and anxiety for their staff.

You are no less employable if you have anxiety. An employer should judge people on their ability to perform the role and nothing more.

Employers cannot discriminate against people because they have anxiety. In most countries it is illegal and if you feel you have suffered unfair treatment you might be able to take legal action.

Does my doctor have to tell my employer I have anxiety?

Neither you nor your doctor (if you have spoken to them) have any requirement to tell your employer that you have an anxiety disorder. Anxiety is a profoundly personal journey and it should be down to each individual to choose if, when and how they wish to share it.

Although there is no requirement to disclose an anxiety disorder, there can be significant benefits in speaking to your employer at a time that feels right for you. Each situation is unique and it is important to use your judgement, seek advice and make a choice that feels right based on your own individual circumstances.

➡️ Are there certain careers better suited to people with anxiety?

It depends on what you love to do! Andy says: 'It wasn't until I was over 40 that I finally found the career that I truly loved and it was amazing how quickly I noticed that it didn't evoke major anxiety within me in the same way as my previous jobs.'

The careers which generate the least anxiety are those that we truly love. In Andy's case it was writing and sharing his story with others through a YouTube channel.

Many people find themselves stuck in jobs they hate and spend endless hours trapped in the cycle of anxiety when they would probably prefer to be doing something else.

So here's the question: *What job would you love to do even if you didn't get paid for doing it?*

If you are unsure, take some time to get clear on your values and explore how well your career choice aligns with them. In many cases people remain in unfulfilling careers that oppose their values and don't realize this is at the core of much of their career-based anxiety.

You may also want to get curious about the times when you feel less anxious and notice how these align with your career choice. For example you might:

- enjoy working alone

- feel fulfilled when you work directly with customers

- enjoy working in a group

- feel rewarded when you get recognition for your efforts

- want regular feedback from your employers.

How can you make changes to your work life so your career starts meeting your needs?

While switching careers or asking for changes to your current role may seem like a momentous task there is nothing to stop you setting some goals and creating a vision board to plan out what you would like to achieve and how you plan to get there. This alone will give you a sense of direction and focus that will instantly make you feel more motivated.

8 low-stress jobs that are perfectly suited to people with anxiety

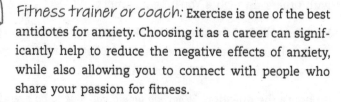

1 *Fitness trainer or coach:* Exercise is one of the best antidotes for anxiety. Choosing it as a career can significantly help to reduce the negative effects of anxiety, while also allowing you to connect with people who share your passion for fitness.

2 *Working in nature:* The outdoors is a natural antidote to stress and anxiety. If you have noticed how much calmer you feel when you connect with nature then you might want to consider a career that takes you outside. There are plenty of roles available, from landscape workers to park rangers, all of which will allow you to find a true sense of fulfilment in nature.

3 *Driving jobs:* Whether it is driving a bus, taxi or delivery truck, many people find the time to themselves far less anxiety-inducing than a career where they are closely monitored or put under significant pressure from supervisors.

4 *Computer work:* Whether writing complex code, building websites or carrying out data entry, computer work can be among the least stressful jobs available. Depending on your role it is often possible to work at your own pace with minimal anxiety triggers around you, although the work can be repetitive at times. For those who enjoy working with computers it can be the perfect low-anxiety career.

5 *Creative work:* Many of the people I work with who experience anxiety problems are incredibly creative and when they tap into this they find it significantly reduces their anxious feelings. Whether you enjoy painting, craft or design, there is sure to be a low-stress career that will suit you.

6 *Bookshop or library:* If you enjoy a quiet work environment and love reading, then working in a bookshop or library could be the ideal anxiety beating career choice for you. You will probably also find that you get time to bury yourself in the latest releases as a wonderful benefit of your role.

7 *Retail/supermarket work:* Many stores need staff to help out of hours to replenish the shelves with stock. This can be a therapeutic and low-stress role for people with anxiety. Depending on your own individual preferences you may also find working in a store where you connect with members of the public will help you feel connected and less anxious.

8 *Charity work:* If money doesn't matter, you might consider volunteering your time to help other people who are less fortunate than you. This can be incredibly rewarding and depending on the people you are working with it can also help you obtain a new sense of perspective around your own problems.

➡️ Can anxiety be a motivator at work?

It might sound counterintuitive, but anxiety can be a motivator at times, especially if we create an intention to harness the positive energy and use it as a tool to push ourselves further.

While it is important to manage the negative symptoms of anxiety, you can also use it to help yourself stay motivated and focused, which in turn can help you achieve more at work and progress your career.

Marisa comments: 'A technique that worked for me was to notice when I was feeling anxious. I would then get really clear on what was behind the anxiety and write down the specifics of the driving force causing the worries and fears within me. Once I knew what was causing my anxiety, I considered if there were any practical steps I could take to help soften the uncomfortable feelings.'

Using Marisa's approach, if for example you are feeling anxious about a work presentation, you might use the feelings as motivation to work on your slides or practice the presentation a few more times to ensure that you feel as confident as possible.

Or if you are feeling anxious about an upcoming meeting that will take you outside your comfort zone, you could practice by doing a role play on your own in front of a mirror.

Instead of attempting to push away any challenging thoughts or feelings, try and take the time to explore them, work out what might be causing them and then ask yourself what practical steps you can take to make yourself feel better.

 Anxiety tip

Write in your journal what you believe may trigger increased anxiety when you are at work. Then explore what steps you can take to minmize the trigger. This might involve asking for more help, requesting additional training or letting go of certain tasks that you don't enjoy for example.

Anxiety in society

Your social situation can play a part in the severity of your symptoms. In this section we will explore the history of anxiety and how society impacts people with a disorder.

➡️ How long has anxiety been around?

Anxiety has likely been in existence for as long as humans have walked on the earth. However, the first documented evidence of anxiety being distinguished as a disorder dates back to Ancient Greek and Latin times.[*]

During the early part of the Renaissance period, women who were experiencing anxiety were believed to be witches, often resulting in extreme consequences such as torture or death.

Things hadn't got much better by time of the Victorian era. Women who showed signs of anxiety continued to be treated as outcasts and were usually labelled as insane before being locked up in a lunatic asylum where they would endure brutal treatment from electroshock therapy to being lobotomized.

During the American Civil War, soldiers were believed to be suffering from what was termed 'irritable heart syndrome' due to their symptoms of anxiety. They were actually suffering what later became known as post-traumatic stress disorder (PTSD).

---

[*] www.ncbi.nlm.nih.gov/pmc/articles/PMC4610616/#:~:text=Naming%20anxiety, word%20is%20angustus%20(narrow)

During this period there was more of an understanding of what anxiety is, but the treatments – which tended to be through the administering of drugs such as opium – were very much short-term solutions.

In the 19th and early 20th centuries, generalized anxiety was known as 'pantophobia' or 'anxiety neurosis', but in the 21st century there has been an increased awareness of the disorder which has resulted in a far better understanding of the problem leading to new treatments and support solutions.

➤ Is anxiety just another label?

Society and humans in general tend to put people into pigeon holes – it makes it easy to quickly work out if another person represents a threat or whether we are safe around them, as well as allowing us to distinguish between different types of people in order to create our own sense of order.

However, labels can also cause us to become stereotyped and people may wrongly assume that because we have been given the 'anxiety' label, it somehow defines who we are and represents everything that we are.

If you tell a child they are stupid over and over, eventually they will believe it and will probably prove you right. I believe that we need to be careful with the use of labels as they can create a sense of stigma, and lead people to internalize the label they have been given, believing they are everything that it says they are.

You can choose whether you want a specific label to apply to you or not – it is your choice and you hold the power. If you don't like a particular label, make a conscious choice not to identify with it.

What does society do to help people with anxiety?

Most societies have become progressively better when it comes to understanding and helping people with anxiety. With as many as one in five people feeling anxious most of the time,* society has an important role to play when it comes to providing support and raising awareness.

Most people are able to find help when they need it, but unless they are aware of the problem they can be held back from seeking support or even knowing where to look. Countries who prioritise the treatment of mental health conditions invest in helping people understand the warning signs of anxiety, overcome fears around stigma and feel comfortable in seeking appropriate help.

Charities and voluntary groups tend to play a major part in the support networks that are available around the world alongside traditional health services.

Many countries are behind the curve when it comes to accepting that they have a problem with anxiety. Even though many in the developed world offer treatment, the number of people accessing it is low when compared to other types of condition, and the standard of care is lacking. Moreover, the problem of mental health issues being seen as a weakness is still an issue globally.†

Societies around the world have a responsibility to continue working on overcoming the ignorance about anxiety through education, and this starts in school classrooms.

---

* https://www.mentalhealth.org.uk/sites/default/files/living-with-anxiety-report. pdf
† https://www.ncbi.nlm.nih.gov/pmc/articles/PMC5553319/

Is anxiety affected by socioeconomic factors?

In short, yes. Just about every country in the world follows the same pattern and while there is no 'one size fits all' for the factors that affect anxiety, there are common themes. Anxiety is not restricted by borders and is prevalent in affluent and poor nations alike. Our gender, age and financial position all have an impact on anxiety, as you will see from the following data.

- People in older age groups tend to be less anxious and more happy.

- Women are more likely to feel anxious than men.

- Only one in twenty people say they never feel anxious.

- Around 20 per cent of people feel anxious most of the time.

- Students and people not in employment are more likely to experience a problem with anxiety than people who are working or retired.

- Around 40 per cent of people in employment experience anxiety about work.

- Around 50 per cent of people who experience anxiety regularly said that financial issues were a significant cause.

- Women and older people are more likely to feel anxious about the wellbeing of a loved one.

- Younger people are more likely to experience anxiety about personal relationships.

- Unemployed people experience significantly higher levels of anxiety.

- Minority ethnic groups experience higher levels of anxiety.

- People with disabilities tend to be more anxious when compared to people with no disabilities.

- Only around 7 per cent of people seek help from their doctor about anxiety, although those who experienced regular anxiety are more likely to do so.

- People who experience regular anxiety tend to feel there is a stigma attached to it.

- Almost 50 per cent of people experience more anxiety now than in the past and feel anxiety has held them back from doing things in their lives. This particularly applies to women and younger people.

While it is almost impossible to know the exact number of people experiencing anxiety disorders around the world, surveys and studies have indicated that the figure is estimated to be 284 million people globally, consisting of approximately 2.7 per cent of men and 4.1 per cent of women. Some studies have shown the figure to be as high as 1 in 5 people experiencing problems with anxiety.[*]

If as many as one out of every five people are experiencing an anxiety disorder, that is around the same chances of catching the flu in a 12-month period. Statistically, you have more chance of developing a problem with anxiety than of:

- missing a soccer penalty kick – 3 in 10 chance

- being left handed – 1 in 10 chance

- having green eyes – 1 in 50 chance

- being killed when involved in a road accident – 1 in 200 chance

- dating a millionaire – 1 in 215 chance

---

[*] All statistics in this section are sourced from: https://www.mentalhealth.org.uk/sites/default/files/living-with-anxiety-report.pdf

- getting divorced – 1 in 250 (based on global averages)

- having twin babies – 1 in 250 chance from natural birth

- finding two yolks in one egg – 1 in 1,000 chance

- being injured while mowing the lawn – 1 in 3,623 chance

- finding a four-leaf clover – 1 in 10,000 chance.

Does where I live affect anxiety?

Very much so, there is a stark contrast in the anxiety rates in different parts of the world. You might be surprised to learn that countries with higher levels of income also have much higher rates of anxiety disorders among their populations.

Studies have also shown that people who live in cities are more likely to face problems with anxiety than people who live in rural areas. Studies have indicated that people who live in a metropolis are 39 per cent more likely to develop an anxiety disorder.*

I have shared some of the headline numbers but do keep in mind that some countries with lower rates of anxiety may be under-estimating their figures due to limitations in recognizing anxiety disorder alongside poor reporting and record keeping processes.

It is worth noting that these figures are taken from a report that shows figures that are lower than the commonly accepted rates of anxiety which are reported to be as high as 20 per cent in parts of the USA. This is because it is based on how many people have been formally diagnosed with a disorder. However, for the purposes of comparing different countries this information is useful.

_____

* https://www.mentalhealth.org.uk/sites/default/files/living-with-anxiety-report.pdf

The discrepancies in accurate data about anxiety also highlights an issue with cohesion and communication that is sure to impact the quality of health services offered in some countries. If governments believe that only 6 per cent of their population are struggling with anxiety, they will provide a level of healthcare to meet the demand. If the real figure is almost four times higher, then they will likely have a mental health time bomb on their hands.

Percentage of the population with anxiety disorders

- New Zealand 8.54%
- Norway 7.59%
- Iran 6.90%
- United States 6.64%
- France 6.63%
- Australia 6.58%
- Uruguay 6.28%
- Italy 5.63%
- Sweden 5.29%
- Canada 5.18%
- Brazil 6.07%
- Spain 5.57%
- United Kingdom 4.65%
- South Africa 3.99%
- Japan 3.57%
- India 3.30%
- Mexico 3.19%
- China 3.03%
- Russia 2.95%
- Nigeria 2.92%
- Columbia 2.51%
- Vietnam 2.07%

Available data shows that:

- West African and Northern Asian nations have among the lowest reported rates of anxiety disorders.

- South African and Northern Asian regions tended to be in the middle of the scale.

- Higher income nations in the Americas, Australasia and Europe have the highest report rates of anxiety disorders.*

While it can be scary to hear medical professionals describing an epidemic around mental health, the reality is that in most countries the figures aren't getting worse and in many locations they have improved as the years have gone by. In addition, reporting is getting better and people are more likely to speak out if they have a problem, which can make the number of cases seem higher when compared to the past.

Anxiety is a problem that affects people globally regardless of where they live. With more people raising awareness about mental health issues and wider access to social media, my belief is that things will continue to improve, and people will experience better access to treatment, and feel more comfortable speaking openly about the challenges they are facing.

 Anxiety tip

Society can condition us to strive for perfection and when we don't achieve it we can feel disheartened which in turn can impact our sense of self-worth. Accept that perfection is not possible and begin to pay attention to how well you have done and how much you have achieved.

---

* All statistics in this section are sourced from https://ourworldindata.org/mental-health#anxiety-disorders

Stigma and shame

In this section, we look at the perception of anxiety by the people who don't suffer it (along with those who do). If you can learn how to reframe your thinking about anxiety while finding suitable connection and support, you can quickly break free from any limiting beliefs that may have held you back in the past.

➡ Is there a stigma around anxiety?

Many people feel a sense of stigma or shame when they suffer from an anxiety disorder and this can cause them to enter a cycle where they end up making their anxiety worse by believing that they are in some way inadequate or unworthy because of the condition they have.

Stigma can be a negative label, used to mark out people who are in some way different and it is often born from ignorance. Some people believe that anxiety is not a real problem; others feel that those with an anxiety disorder are seeking attention or should just be able to snap themselves out of it.

When we listen to the stories that other people have created based on their own limiting beliefs and life experiences, we can end up allowing ourselves to be sucked into their version of the truth about anxiety.

While stigma is not classed as discrimination, it is very similar. By being sure that you are proud of who you are, and understanding that there is no shame in anxiety, you will be able to write your own story.

You can help yourself by:

- setting boundaries with people who make you feel bad about yourself, even if this means cutting contact with them
- asking for help when you need it and knowing where to get it
- getting the facts about anxiety and having a clear understanding of how it impacts people around the world
- surrounding yourself with positive people who are on the same journey towards healing anxiety and understand the challenges you are facing
- writing daily in your journal
- learning to notice and name your feelings and emotions and expressing them whenever it is appropriate to do so
- practising speaking your truth and saying what you really feel when appropriate.

Society has woken up to mental health in the last decade and attitudes are changing. While there may be some people who believe that anxiety should carry with it a sense of stigma and shame, that is simply their view of the world – you have no obligation to share what they believe.

▶ Can shame cause anxiety?

There is no such thing as a 'bad' feeling or emotion. Feelings are with us for a reason and part of our job as humans is to look at them and question them, rather than causing ourselves more pain by pushing them away, or trying to avoid them.

What we try to resist will persist – I learned this the hard way by spending decades trying to stay as far away as possible from my own feelings. It was only when I began to face them that I began to make real progress.

At the root of almost all of the feelings that lead to anxious thought patterns is toxic shame. You are likely to be holding toxic shame if:

- you have a sense that you are in some way not good enough, unworthy or inadequate

- you grew up in a household where feelings were not shown or shared and emotions were withheld

- you justify your feelings of shame and have a story to explain why you are inadequate or unworthy

- you struggle with criticism, even when it is meant to be constructive or helpful

- you feel inadequate and compare yourself to other people; this might be through comparison of your body, career or relationships, for example

- you experience angry outbursts and direct aggressive reactions to either yourself or people around you

- you struggle to connect with your feelings and emotions – you might be unable to get angry or find that you rarely cry, for example

- you put other people on a pedestal and idealize them – you might believe that someone else has a better life than you because you think they are more attractive, intelligent or successful than you, for example

- you feel as though you do not deserve success or good things in your life

- you often strive for the next thing in your life in the belief that everything will be better when you achieve it (or buy it, in the case of striving for material possessions)

- you overcompensate for your shame by people-pleasing, being overly nice or apologizing even if you have done nothing wrong

- you struggle to speak your mind and be truly authentic, you might find you have different versions of yourself and personas that you show to the world depending on the specific situation

- you experience negative or shame based self-talk such as 'I am a bad person', 'nobody could ever love me' or 'I will never amount to anything'.

Toxic shame is at the very heart of many of the issues surrounding anxiety. It has its roots in emotional neglect and trauma in childhood. While you may not instantly identify with these as part of your own life, they can be incredibly subtle yet have a profound impact in adulthood.

If you have spotted any signs that you might be carrying toxic shame, I invite you to read my book *How To Heal Your Inner Child* (Sheldon Press, 2021) in order to explore further and gently unpackage what you are holding so you can start to move forward feeling lighter and free.

Are there any groups or communities for people with anxiety?

Abi says: 'One of the biggest things that helped me overcome my own anxiety was connecting with people who understood what I was going through and were on the same journey. Yes, it helps to draw on the support available from friends and family, but there's nothing that compares to the power you can draw on from other people who have the same shared experiences.'

By connecting with other people on the same journey you can learn from those who have made progress and overcome the obstacles they have been presented with by their anxiety disorder. By finding a mentor or role model you can feel accountable to someone and significantly increase your chances of successfully reducing your anxiety.

There are numerous groups and communities for people with anxiety and some of the best groups can be found on social media websites such as Facebook and Instagram. Most of the Facebook groups are private which means you can interact in confidence that none of your other online friends can see anything you post.

Try joining a few groups so you can start immersing yourself in them. You will probably make new friends and find that your mindset shifts to a place of positivity and belief in yourself.

You can find a list of some of the best groups to join in the Resources section later in this book.

Is anxiety good for you?

You might be shocked to learn that anxiety can be good for you, although of course, on the whole, the negative impact can outweigh any upsides. That said, if you can tap into the positive aspects of being overly anxious you can channel the energy rather like a superpower that will enable you to achieve more and go further than those who do not possess the same gift.

Anxiety can be good for you when you need to:

- *Feel motivated*: Anxious feelings can spur us to get things done, especially when we have fears about a negative outcome that might happen if we don't take action. Although the thoughts and feelings are uncomfortable, they can be a huge driving force when it comes to feeling motivated.

- **Be well prepared**: Anxious people tend to go the extra mile when it comes to preparing themselves. This might be for a public talk, a presentation or a big meeting at work for example, when we are anxious we usually have fears about the potential negative consequences that could arise if we don't meet our own expectations or those of others. As a result, anxious people are experts at preparation and practicing to ensure they perform at their very best when they need to shine.

- **Stay focused**: When we are anxious about an event or situation that is important to us, we will spend more time focusing on it. People with heightened anxiety will often play through different scenarios and seek out solutions to problems with creative thinking. During these times they will experience a sharpened sense of focus and will likely not rest until they have settled their inner fears.

- **Feel safe**: Anxiety is rooted in fear. Although the fears are often irrational they are ultimately with us to ensure we feel safe and protected. As a result, anxious people tend to keep themselves safe, weigh up risks and avoid situations that might put them in danger and many have what they might consider a sixth sense when it comes to avoiding risky situations and danger.

- **Be authentic**: Anxious people often feel compelled to share their uncomfortable thoughts and feelings with others, often to provide themselves with a sense of reassurance. In doing so they are able to create a deep level of connection with others and are able to be totally real and honest about their feelings and emotions, which many people find incredibly hard to do.

When you feel anxious in the future try to avoid instantly assuming it is a bad thing; the feelings are often with us for a good reason and may contain an important message that requires your attention. If you can begin to see some of the ways that anxiety can be good for you, and assist you in overcoming challenges, you might realize that in some respects, anxiety can be a gift.

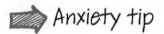 Anxiety tip

Can you find a pattern in what causes you to feel shame and what triggers anxious feelings? Use a journal to write down the potential sources of these feelings and consider what steps you could take to prevent them.

Breaking the cycle of anxiety

In this final section, we examine exactly what you can do in order to overcome anxiety and start living the life you deserve. This section provides you with tips, tools and tactics that will help you set yourself up to make a change and move forward.

How many people have overcome anxiety?

Anxiety impacts tens of millions of people around the world with estimates indicating that more than forty million people in the United States and more than eight million in the United Kingdom have anxiety-related problems, and as many as one in four children aged between 13 and 18 also find themselves dealing with an anxiety disorder.[*]

It's very easy to believe that anxiety is your destiny, and that there's little to no point trying to change that. Evidence suggests that more than 60 per cent of people receive no diagnosis or treatment for their anxiety disorder. In fact, there has never been more support available and it is very possible to beat anxiety if you become motivated to do so.

---

[*] https://www.weforum.org/agenda/2019/01/this-is-the-worlds-biggest-mental-health-problem/#:~:text=goes%20to%20anxiety.-,An%20estimated%20275%20million%20people%20suffer%20from%20anxiety%20disorders.,with%20105%20million%20male%20sufferers

Anxiety treatment is usually very effective and can range from talking therapy to medication. While there are no statistics that show how many people make a full recovery from anxiety it is believed that around one in three people with an anxiety disorder seek treatment and a vast number of these are able to reach a place where the condition is no longer causing significant problems in their life.

The worst thing you can do when you have anxiety is nothing. You can overcome it, but this might take time and persistence – in many cases recovery is a journey of finding what works through trial and error. Don't allow any setbacks to put you off, simply learn from them, work out what you need to do differently and continue moving along the path towards healing.

Is there one thing that can fix anxiety?

We are all complex creatures made up of many different parts. What works for one person may not work for another and it is important to be mindful of this when you begin exploring what might help you overcome an anxiety disorder.

Tobi says: 'There was one technique that worked incredibly well for me and it involved me scheduling a time to meet with my worries and fears. Instead of allowing my anxious thoughts to derail me whenever they pleased, I set aside a time each morning where I would meet with my worries. I called this my "worry time". My worry time started at 8:30am and finished promptly at 9am. If I had an anxious thought outside this time, I'd stick it in my mental to-do tray and tell it firmly that I was not prepared to engage right now; it would have to wait for our scheduled meeting the next day. When the time for our morning meeting came, I'd sit in front of the mirror and talk to myself about my worries. Suddenly they stopped seeming so powerful, and I always came out of "worry time" feeling lighter and less anxious; often I would have made decisions about anything that I might need to do.'

This technique worked for Tobi because it allowed them to let go of their worries because they hadn't attempted to ignore them, they had simply moved them to one side with the intention of addressing them when they were ready, on their time and on their terms.

Why don't you give Tobi's method a try? You might be surprised at how effective it is, and how much more in control you will feel.

As well as techniques like scheduling worry time, there are also more common treatments you can explore for anxiety.

The most effective treatments for anxiety disorders include:

Cognitive behavioural therapy (CBT)

CBT aims to change the way people view their problems by breaking them down into smaller, more manageable parts. In doing so it becomes possible to make more sense of them and change the subsequent reactions.

Through CBT work problems are broken down into five different areas:

- actions
- emotions
- physical feelings and sensations
- situations
- thoughts.

Unlike psychotherapy, CBT takes a structured approach and identifies specific problems and challenges that are causing issues and then guides people to help themselves by finding appropriate solutions that will end negative responses.

The essence of CBT is around adopting a different mindset and a more positive and pragmatic viewpoint. If you have just lost your job for example, instead of wallowing in self-pity, calling yourself a failure and giving up on ever finding a new role, CBT will help you understand that many people change careers and there are countless opportunities available for you if you learn from any mistakes and keep moving forward. You might work with your therapist as you formulate a plan of action and will likely feel far more positive once you know what you need to do to launch into the new chapter of your career.

Emotional freedom technique (EFT)

EFT is also known as tapping or psychological acupressure and is used to treat a wide range of physical and emotional problems. Research is still in the early stages, but there is evidence to demonstrate that EFT can quickly dissipate strong anxious feelings.*

Similar to acupuncture, the process of tapping focuses on the meridian points of the body to disrupt negative energy. Meridian points were introduced in Chinese medicine and are believed to be the areas of the body where energy flows the strongest.

Instead of using needles, EFT involves using the hands and fingers to tap on the energy hot spots which in turn sends signals to the parts of the brain that control stress. The process can quickly rebalance any negativity.

I often use tapping techniques and have found them to be incredibly powerful. There are several apps that can guide you through the process and plenty of specialists who will introduce you to the process required to bring this helpful tool into your anti-anxiety armoury.

---

* https://www.therecoveryvillage.com/mental-health/anxiety/related/eft-tapping/#:~:text=EFT%20tapping%20therapy%20has%20been,sleeping%20difficulties%20and%20difficulty%20concentrating.

Relaxation techniques

Relaxation techniques help calm the mind and body and allow people to soften difficult thoughts and feelings by focusing on inner sensations and the present moment.

Popular techniques that are proven to reduce stress when practised regularly include breathwork, mindfulness, yoga, meditation and visualization.

There are numerous apps, videos, books and guides to assist if you are interested in exploring relaxation techniques. See the Resources section at the back of this book for more information.

SSRI medication

Selective serotonin reuptake inhibitors (SSRIs) work by powering up the communication between neurotransmitters in the brain. When we experience problems with stress, anxiety and depression it is often linked to poor communication when the brain sends chemical messages and signals from one place to another.

Think of it like a mobile phone in your brain – when you send a message via text only part of the message is received by the recipient, and as a result they cannot follow the instructions in the message and don't act on them correctly.

SSRI medication gives users a proper signal that allows the communication system to work correctly in the parts of the brain that regulate emotion and mood.

SNRI medication

Serotonin and norepinephrine inhibitors (SNRIs) work by stabilizing neurotransmitters in the brain to ensure a smooth flow of communication, similar to SSRI medication.

What makes them different from SSRI medication is the fact that SNRIs work by influencing serotonin and norepinephrine, which are both neurotransmitters that can impact mood and feelings of anxiety. SSRIs only influence serotonin.

Pregabalin medication

Pregabalin is most commonly used as an anti-epilepsy drug but is also prescribed to treat a range of symptoms including anxiety, fibromyalgia, neuropathic pain and restless leg syndrome.

It works by slowing down impulses in the brain and maintaining a balance in the nervous system which helps to relieve anxious feelings.

Benzodiazepine medication

Benzodiazepines are often referred to as 'benzos' and they help with anxiety by raising the level of GABA (gamma aminobutyric acid) in the brain which serves to slow the person down leading to a calm, or even sedative state.

Finding your own 'therapies'

Some people prefer to curate their own form of therapy by understanding what makes them feel good. When we are engaging in something that brings us true joy and happiness it helps to eliminate negative feelings and makes us feel good through the release of dopamine.

The process is fairly simple, and the goal is to follow your joy by identifying what takes you to a blissful state.

Think about the hobbies, pastimes and activities you do now (or did when you were younger). Which of them make hours feel like minutes? Consider what causes you to become so immersed in what you are doing you literally lose track of time

– these activities are the gateway to you finding your own form of therapy through doing what you love.

Spend more time following your joy: we all owe it to ourselves to follow the path that calls us.

The power of the now

Something that is hugely helpful in reducing anxiety is working on becoming fully present in the moment and disabling yourself from becoming entangled in thoughts about the past or future. Your mind is, simply, a tool that at times can be very useful – but it is not all of you, and it is important that you don't rely on using only this single tool to run your life. Just know that you can take it out of your toolbox anytime you like, but until you need it, make a choice to keep it quiet and still.

Whenever we are fully present and in the now it is much harder to feel anxious, and much easier to feel connected, joyful and light.

Try it today. Every time you find your mind wandering or your thoughts racing about anything that is not in the present moment, observe it without judgement and bring yourself back to the now. You will know your mind is in an unhelpful place when it is focused on the past or the future.

The more you practise this technique, the more natural it will become and you will soon find that you are significantly less anxious and far more connected to the world around you. Try reading the book *The Power of Now: A Guide to Spiritual Enlightenment* by Eckhart Tolle (see the Resources section) if you would like to explore how being more present can eradicate anxious feelings.

➡️ How can I stop a panic attack?

Panic attacks may appear out of the blue and catch us when we least expect them. It is not always possible to stop them and, in fact, it is better to surf the uncomfortable feelings until they pass instead of trying to resist – when we attempt to fight an impending panic attack it often becomes worse.

With practice it is possible to feel more in control during these uncomfortable episodes and at the same time you can remove much of the power from what may have previously been a totally overwhelming experience.

➡️ How to reduce the strength of a panic attack

Use an anchoring technique

Anchoring can help you change unwanted feelings to positivity in a matter of moments by creating a stimulus response pattern that will trigger the desired outcome.

It is essentially a form of mental reconditioning which works by creating an association between a stimulus and a positive feeling or thought.

To try anchoring for yourself follow these steps:

 1 Decide how you want to feel and create a mantra that you can easily remember. It is important that your mantra is something you know to be true. For example, 'I know a panic attack always passes, it cannot hurt me, I am safe.'

2 Think hard about the truth around your statement, gather evidence that proves it is absolutely true. In this example you might reflect on past panic attacks and remember how quickly a panic attack passed while reminding yourself that you were safe at all times during the episode. Try to get really clear on this, the more vividly you can visualize experiences that reinforce your statement in step one to be true, the better the process will work.

 3 Decide on what stimulus will trigger you to be able to feel and experience your statement in step one. Anchoring works best when you inflict a small amount of pain on yourself as this instantly allows the new positive feelings to wash over you. This could be pinching your hand or digging a nail into your thumb for example.

4 Say the statement in step one out loud, it helps if you look into your own eyes by doing it in front of a mirror. Directly after you have spoken the statement you should make the stimulus action you have chosen, such as pinching your hand. Repeat the process at least twenty times and continue repeating it over the next week until you feel like it has stuck.

5 When you are faced with a panic attack you can use your stimulus to trigger the outcome you want.

Get comfortable and breathe

If you're experiencing a panic attack, try to avoid breathing too quickly. Instead, focus your attention on your breath and breathe in and out slowly through your nose, observing the flow of air as it passes in and out of your body.

If you can, find a position that feels really comfortable, either lying on a bed or sitting with your head between your legs, for example. Think about what position makes you feel safest – this is often the one that serves us best.

Slow and focused breathing will not stop a panic attack. The goal is to breathe *through* the episode and minimize the impact it has, do not attempt to fight or push it away, allow it to be with you in the knowledge that you are safe and it will pass.

Practising breathing exercises regularly will improve your ability to stay focused on your breath during challenging episodes instead of being drawn into them.

Remain fully present

Whether you realize it or not, panic attacks are often manifestations of our fears about the past or the future. If you focus on remaining in the present moment, you can simply observe what is happening rather than become a participant in the mental drama.

A method for staying present during a panic attack:

 Notice five things you can see and say them out loud, or write them down.

 Notice four things you can touch, then touch them and say them out loud or write them down.

 Notice three things you can hear, listen to them carefully, say them out loud or write them down.

 Notice two things you can smell. Experience the aroma then say them out loud or write them down.

 Notice one thing you can taste. If possible, savour the taste, then say it out loud or write it down.

Shake it out

Panic attacks are linked to our nervous system and vigorous shaking can get things back on track when it has become dysregulated.

If you notice the warning signs of a panic attack try regulating your nervous system by vigorously shaking one hand, then one foot, then repeating with the other hand and foot.

This causes an instant disruption to the nervous system and can significantly reduce the strength of a panic attack. Try to practice this technique when you feel low level anxiety rather than waiting until you have a more powerful episode.

Again, it is important to be clear that we are not attempting to fight a panic attack. The goal is to acknowledge it is with you in that moment, stay present, regulate your breathing and nervous system, before allowing it to pass.

Do antidepressants help anxiety?

Antidepressants can help people feel calmer and more equipped to deal with their problems, challenges and any worrying thoughts they may be experiencing. However, everyone has a different experience with medication and what works for some people may make others feel worse. It is essential that you consult a suitably qualified medical professional before deciding on what might be right for you.

Whether or not you are discussing antidepressants with your doctor, do take the time to consider what other aspects of your lifestyle may be causing anxiety, including such triggers as:

- stress from work
- moving home or changes in your living environment
- problems in your relationship
- family problems
- emotional shock or trauma from a stressful event

- alcohol

- diet and nutrition

- verbal, physical or sexual abuse

- conception, pregnancy, and/or giving birth

- physical illness.

How do these areas of your life look right now? If you don't feel content in a specific area, consider what you could change to make your own life more peaceful and happier.

If you do choose to use antidepressants, ensure you carefully track how you feel each day using an app or your journal, this data will be crucial in determining whether the medication has improved your symptoms or made them worse. Ask your doctor how long it should take to see an improvement and continue to track how you feel for at least 12 months to monitor anything that might occur while you're taking them.

▶ Can anxiety be treated naturally?

Research has indicated that supplements can help to relieve anxiety symptoms.* However, it is important to note that not all supplements are effective and some may not be suitable for you. For many people it is a case of trial and error and it is essential to track the data as you perform your own supplement clinical trials on yourself. Try recording your mood, logging any anxiety attacks and tracking your supplement intake using an app or your journal. Once you have gathered enough data you can make a firm decision about what works best for you based on solid evidence.

---

* https://www.healthline.com/nutrition/supplements-for-anxiety#our-picks

7 supplements that may help to relieve the symptoms of anxiety

1 Vitamin D: This been proven to play a role in mood regulation as well as helping to boost the immune system and brain function. Studies have shown that vitamin D can also reduce anxiety. Exposing the body to natural sunlight is a great way to absorb vitamin D, it can also be found in fatty fish or taken as a supplement.

2 Magnesium: This mineral plays a vital role in managing stress responses; research has shown that it also has benefits when it comes to reducing anxiety. It can be found in green vegetables, grains, nuts, seeds, wheat and bran. You can also buy over-the-counter magnesium supplements.

3 Omega-3 fatty acids: These can be found in oily fish, nuts and seeds or taken as supplements. These acids play a crucial role in brain health and recent studies have backed up claims that increasing the amount of omega-3 in the body can reduce anxiety. It is important to get the dosage correct, some people require high doses to experience an effect. It is worth speaking to your doctor or a suitably qualified specialist to get an expert opinion.

4 Saffron: Commonly used in cooking, this brightly coloured spice is packed with antioxidants that are believed to help people with anxiety. Studies have shown that saffron has similar anti-anxiety benefits to some of the most popular prescription medications. Saffron can be taken as a supplement.

5 Lavender: Smelling lavender has been shown to induce a feeling of relaxation, and some people have reported using lavender to ease anxiety and overcome panic attacks.

6 *Chamomile*: This is best known as a tea and renowned for its calming benefits. However it is also thought to reduce anxiety and studies have indicated that chamomile supplements can have a positive impact on people struggling with anxious feelings.

7 *L-theanine*: This has been shown to decrease cortisol levels and reduce anxious responses and feelings, evidence has indicated that it acts as a mild sedative and has anti-anxiety properties. It can be found in green and black tea or taken as a supplement.

As well as considering supplements as a method of naturally treating anxiety, it is also important to review your diet and lifestyle and pay attention to what foods or activities may be having a negative impact.

Read the ingredients and labels on your food, especially if you buy pre-prepared or packaged meals. Over time you can create an anti-anxiety nutrition plan that will help boost your mood and regulate your anxiety.

Rajinder says: 'As a former junk food eater who has beaten anxiety, I now try and stick to foods with limited numbers of healthy ingredients. If my grandmother wouldn't eat it, cook with it or recognize an ingredient on the label, then it is probably best for me to avoid it. This test has really helped me to improve my diet, and that has played an important role in managing my anxiety.'

It is so helpful to look at your diet and create an anxiety-beating nutrition plan. Some people have completely eliminated anxiety by making simple changes and food swaps alone.

➡️ What to avoid in your diet:

- *Sugary drinks*: Food and drink that contain high amounts of sugar cause a spike in blood sugar levels. These spikes have been linked to anxiety. Sugary drinks can contain as much as 15 teaspoons of sugar in a single can, which can cause huge spikes followed by a feeling of anxious crashing.

- *Artificial sweeteners*: Artificial sweeteners have been directly linked to neuropsychiatric problems including anxiety. While some people may be unaffected by sweeteners, others may encounter a significant impact. If you are unable to avoid sweeteners try to minimize your intake or experiment by taking a break and gathering data around what changes you experience.

- *Stealth sugars*: Many products contain hidden sugars, even if they are marketed as savoury. These stealth sugars can have a negative impact on anxiety and it is important to pay close attention to what you are consuming as people often don't realize how much hidden sugar is in their food.

- *Foods containing gluten*: Evidence suggests that gluten may be linked to heightened anxiety in some people and it is another area of your diet that you could try experimenting with so you can discover what changes.

- *Caffeine, including tea, coffee and energy drinks*: The more caffeine you put into your body, the more you increase the chances of experiencing heightened levels of anxiety. Caffeine stimulates the adenosine receptors in the nervous system, adenosine helps to manage our fight, flight or freeze response and is directly linked to how anxious we feel.

- *Foods high in sugar such as cakes and cookies*: Foods with high sugar content have the ability to cause problems with anxiety. Wherever possible try and minimize your intake. Eating high sugar foods regularly can cause numerous health problems including weight gain, which – rightly or wrongly – can lead to worsened social anxiety and exacerbate pre-existing problems.

- **Fermented foods**: Although fermented foods like sauerkraut and kimchi are great for gut health, they have also been linked to anxiety and panic attacks in some people. This is due to the presence of the histamines created during the fermentation process. Excess histamines can create feelings of panic as well as brain inflammation that causes anxiety.

- **Processed foods**: Processed foods are right up there with the worst choices to have on your plate at mealtime if you want to reduce anxiety. Most contain hidden sugars and high sodium levels which cause inflammatory responses in the body leading to changes in the parts of the brain that control arousal, anxiety and alarm.

- **Nicotine**: Nicotine creates a short-term sense of relaxation, which can cause smokers to believe that the habit reduces anxiety. However, research has shown that smoking increases stress and anxiety and as soon as the short-term effects subside they are replaced by cravings for more.*

- **Alcohol**: It's not an exaggeration to say that drinking alcohol can be like pouring fuel on the fire of anxiety. Not only does alcohol cause sugar spikes, it impacts almost every area of the mind and body and causes havoc when it comes to anxious feelings. Many people drink because they believe alcohol calms anxiety and don't pay attention to how much worse they feel after drinking.

Many people do notice a big drop in their anxiety levels when they cut out alcohol. Try taking a break from drinking for a month or two and you will likely notice a significant difference.

---

* https://www.mentalhealth.org.uk/a-to-z/s/smoking-and-mental-health#:~:text=Smoking%20and%20stress,it%20reduces%20stress%20and%20anxiety.

➡ Anxiety tip

Create a support network of trusted friends and family members who you can talk to when you're feeling anxious or overwhelmed. If you find it difficult to reach out to people you know, take the time to find a therapist or counsellor who can support you in complete confidence.

FAQs

1 About anxiety
What is anxiety, exactly?
How do I know I have a problem with anxiety?
What are the signs that someone has anxiety?
Are there different types of anxiety?
Do I have to be formally diagnosed with anxiety, or can I diagnose myself?
What is the difference between anxiety and depression? (and will I get depression too?)

2 Living with anxiety
How can I live with an anxiety disorder?
Are there things I shouldn't do if I feel anxious?
How is anxiety impacted my lifestyle?
Can hobbies and pastimes reduce anxiety?
Does having anxiety make me an introvert?
Should I tell people I have anxiety?
Are there good habits that help reduce anxiety?
Can non-anxiety medication make things worse?
What foods help reduce anxiety (and which ones make it worse)?
Can my choice of clothing and furniture help reduce symptoms?
What else can make anxiety worse?
Does quality of sleep have a bearing on anxiety?

3 The emotional side of anxiety
Is anxiety a type of emotion?
How can I tell the difference between anxiety and fear?
Is anxiety linked to trauma?
How does anxiety affect my emotional wellbeing?
What does an anxiety attack feel like?
Can an anxiety attack cause a heart attack?
Why is my brain constantly racing with thoughts?

Are people with anxiety negative thinkers?

Can anxiety affect my memory?

Can anxiety lead to addiction?

Are people with anxiety more likely to engage in risky behaviour?

What is the best way of managing difficult emotions?

4 The physical cost of anxiety

What is the link between anxiety and the human body?

How can anxiety affect me physically?

Can anxiety weaken my immune system?

Does anxiety increase blood pressure?

Does anxiety increase the risk of cancer?

Can anxiety cause hair loss?

Is anxiety impacted by my weight?

Is anxiety linked to gut health?

How many people die because of anxiety?

Does the nervous system control anxiety?

5 Anxiety and relationships

How does anxiety affect a relationship?

Do people with anxiety struggle to form relationships?

Will anxiety make me a bad parent?

Can anxiety affect my sex life?

Can my partner help me eliminate anxiety?

Are people with anxiety more likely to end up alone?

Will anxiety cause problems if I want to become a parent?

6 Anxiety at work

Can anxiety hold me back in my career?

What is performance anxiety?

Are people with anxiety less employable?

Does my doctor have to tell my employer I have anxiety?

Are there certain careers better suited to people with anxiety?

Can anxiety be a motivator at work?

7 Anxiety in society

How long has anxiety been around?

Is anxiety just another label?

What does society do to help people with anxiety?

Is anxiety affected by socioeconomic factors?

Does where I live affect anxiety?

8 Stigma and shame

Is there a stigma around anxiety?

Can shame cause anxiety?

Are there any groups or communities for people with anxiety?

Is anxiety good for you?

9 Breaking the cycle of anxiety

How many people have overcome anxiety?

Is there one thing that can fix anxiety?

How can I stop a panic attack?

Do antidepressants help anxiety?

Can anxiety be treated naturally?

Resources

Recommended reading

David Carbonell (2016) *The Worry Trick: How Your Brain Tricks You into Expecting the Worst and What You Can Do about It* (New Harbinger)

Edmund J. Bourne (2020) *The Anxiety and Phobia Workbook* (New Harbinger)

Lucinda Bassett (1997) *From Panic to Power* (William Morrow & Company)

Eckhart Tolle (2010) *The Power of Now: A Guide to Spiritual Enlightenment* (New World Library)

David Burns (2007) *When Panic Attacks: The New Drug-Free Anxiety Therapy That Can Change Your Life* (Broadway Books)

Trudy Scott (2011) *The Anti-Anxiety Food Solution* (New Harbinger)

Scott Stossel (2014) *My Age of Anxiety* (Windmill Books)

Barry McDonagh (2015) *Dare: The New Way To End Anxiety And Stop Panic Attacks* (BMD Publishing)

Support groups

Anxiety Anonymous – www.adaa.org

Daily Strength – www.dailystrength.org/group/anxiety

7 Cups – www.7cups.com

Support Groups Central – www.supportgroupscentral.com

Mental Health America – www.mhanational.org

Support Groups – www.supportgroups.com

The Tribe – support.therapytribe.com

Anxiety Central – www.anxiety-central.com

 # Organizations

Anxiety and Depression Association of America (ADAA) –
www.adaa.org
Anxiety UK – www.anxietyuk.org.uk
Mind – www.mind.org.uk
Social Anxiety Association – www.socialphobia.org
SANE – www.sane.org.uk

Websites

Anxiety United – www.anxietyunited.com
Anxiety Slayer – www.anxietyslayer.com
The Anxiety Guy – www.theanxietyguy.com
Elephant Journal – www.elephantjournal.com
The Mighty – www.themighty.com
Beautiful Voyager – www.bevoya.com

Apps

Self-Help for Anxiety Management (SAM) – Anxiety manage-
ment tools
Pacifica – Anxiety management tools
MoodMission – Strategies, games and rewards for managing
anxiety
Insight Timer – Free meditation, sleep and relaxation
Headspace – Meditation, mindfulness and sleep
Calm – Meditation, relaxation and stress relief
iMoodJournal – Mood tracking and monitoring
Colorfy – Adult colouring app for relaxation
Breathwrk – Breathing techniques
Moodnotes – Journalling
Mindshift – Cognitive behaviour therapy (CBT)
ReachOut Breath – Breath control and breathing techniques

YouTube Channels for Videos

Anxiety United
The Anxiety Guy
Kati Morton
WonderBro
Bignoknow
Living with Health Anxiety
Psych Hub
The Psych Show
Anxiety Canada
Depression to Expression
Beyond Blue Official
Dr Rami Nader
Psych to Go

Podcasts

The Calmer You Podcast
Your Anxiety Toolkit
The Anxiety Slayer
Not Another Anxiety Show
Rebele Buddhist
Being Well
The Anxiety Coaches
10% Happier
The Overwhelmed Brain
The Anxiety Guy
The One You Feed